HEALING A BROKEN HEART

A Journey from Pain to Peace

HENRY ABRAHAMS

assume any responsibility for third-party websites or their content that may be linked to from within this book.

ISBN: 9798327164468

Table of Contents

Introduction

Heartbreak is a universal experience that knows no boundaries. It transcends age, culture, and background, affecting everyone at some point in their lives. Whether it's the end of a romantic relationship, the loss of a loved one, or a deep disappointment, the pain of a broken heart can feel overwhelming. This book is dedicated to those who are going through the tumultuous waters of heartbreak, offering guidance, support, and hope.

When we're in the throes of heartache,

it often feels like the world has come to a standstill. The future seems bleak, and the present is colored by a deep sense of loss and sorrow. The emotional toll can be immense, leading to feelings of sadness, anger, confusion, and even despair. It's important to acknowledge these feelings as a natural part of the healing process. In understanding that heartbreak is a shared human experience, we begin to see that we are not alone in our suffering.

The Journey to Healing

Healing a broken heart is a journey, not a destination. It is a process that unfolds over time, requiring patience, self-compassion, and resilience. This book is designed to be a companion on that journey, providing practical advice, emotional support, and a roadmap to recovery. Each book is crafted to address different aspects of the healing process, from accepting the pain to rediscovering joy and embracing new beginnings.

The path to healing is rarely linear. There will be moments of progress and setbacks, days when the pain feels manageable and days when it seems unbearable. This is all part of the journey. The key is to keep moving forward, even if it's just one small step at a time.

A Personal Note

As someone who has experienced the depths of heartbreak, I understand how isolating and consuming it can be. I wrote this book not only from a place of empathy but also from a desire to share the insights and tools that helped me find my way back to wholeness. My hope is that through these pages, you will find comfort, strength, and a renewed sense of hope.

This book is not about quick fixes or unrealistic promises. It's about real, tangible steps you can take to heal your heart and reclaim your life. It's about learning to care for yourself, to honor your emotions, and to rebuild your sense of self-worth. Most importantly, it's about finding the courage to open your heart to love again, in whatever form that may take.

Navigating This Book

Each chapter of this book is designed to stand alone, allowing you to dip in and out as needed. Whether you're just beginning your healing journey or are well on your way, you can find chapters that resonate with your current state of mind. The exercises, reflections, and practical tips are meant to be adaptable to your unique situation.

Take your time with this book. Healing is a deeply personal process, and there is no right or wrong way to go about it. Allow yourself the grace to move at your own pace, and remember that every small step you take is a victory in itself.

As you embark on this journey, know that you are not alone. Countless others have walked this path before you and have found their way to the other side. You, too, can heal your broken heart and emerge stronger, wiser, and more resilient than ever before.

Welcome to your healing journey. Let's take the first step together.

Chapter 1

Accepting the Pain

- ## The Importance of Acknowledgement

The first step in healing a broken heart is often the hardest: acknowledging the pain. In a society that frequently urges us to "stay strong" and "move on," admitting that we are hurting can feel like a radical act. Yet, it is an essential part of the healing process. Without acknowledgment, pain festers, hiding in the shadows of our consciousness and manifesting in ways that can affect our emotional and physical well-being.

Acknowledging your pain means facing it head-on. It means allowing yourself to feel the full weight of your emotions, without judgment or suppression. This can be a daunting prospect, especially when every fiber of your being wants to escape the discomfort. However, by acknowledging your pain, you validate your experience and give yourself permission to heal.

Why Acknowledgement Matters

When we refuse to acknowledge our pain, we inadvertently prolong our suffering. Unaddressed emotions can lead to a range of issues, including anxiety, depression, and even physical illness. The act of acknowledgment is a way of telling ourselves that our feelings are real and that they matter. It's a form of self-validation that sets the stage for genuine healing.

Acknowledgment is not just about admitting that we are in pain; it's about understanding the source of that pain. This can involve reflecting on the relationship or event that caused the heartbreak, recognizing what was lost, and appreciating the impact it has had on our lives. This process of reflection can be painful, but it is necessary for us to move forward.

Practical Steps to Acknowledge Your Pain

1. Create a Safe Space:

Find a quiet, comfortable place where you can be alone with your thoughts. This could be a cozy corner of your home, a peaceful spot in nature, or anywhere you feel secure. Creating a safe environment is crucial for allowing yourself to be vulnerable.

2. Journal Your Feelings:

Writing can be a powerful tool for processing emotions. Take some time each day to journal about your feelings. Write freely, without worrying about grammar or coherence. Let the words flow as they come. This exercise can help you articulate your pain and gain clarity on your emotions.

3. Speak It Out:

Sometimes, verbalizing our pain can be even more cathartic than writing. Talk to a trusted friend, family member, or therapist about what you're going through. Saying the words out loud can make your feelings more tangible and real, and the support from others can provide comfort.

4. Accept Your Emotions:

Understand that it's okay to feel hurt, angry, sad, or confused. These emotions are natural responses to loss. Give yourself permission to feel them fully. Avoid the temptation to downplay or dismiss your feelings. Every emotion has its place in the healing process.

5. Meditate on Your Feelings:

Mindfulness meditation can be a helpful practice for sitting with your emotions without judgment. Spend a few minutes each day focusing on your breath and observing your thoughts and feelings as they arise. Acknowledge each emotion with compassion, then let it pass without clinging to it.

The Healing Power of Acknowledgement

Acknowledging your pain is a courageous act of self-love. It shows that you respect your emotions and are willing to take the necessary steps to heal. By facing your pain, you begin to dismantle the power it holds over you. This doesn't mean the pain will disappear overnight, but it does mean that you are actively engaging in your healing process.

Over time, this acknowledgment can lead to profound insights and personal growth. You may start to understand patterns in your relationships, recognize areas where you need to set healthier boundaries, or discover new aspects of yourself that were previously hidden. Each of these insights is a stepping stone on the path to recovery.

In acknowledging your pain, you are not only validating your past experiences but also paving the way for a brighter future. You are telling yourself that it's okay to hurt, and it's okay to take the time you need to heal. This compassionate approach will serve as the foundation for all the steps that follow in your healing journey.

Remember, you are not alone in this process. Countless others have walked this path and emerged stronger and more resilient. By acknowledging your pain, you are taking the first, vital step toward joining them in the light of recovery.

- **Allowing Yourself to Grieve**

Grief is a natural response to loss, and when it comes to heartbreak, allowing yourself to grieve is crucial. Grieving is not a sign of weakness but a testament to the depth of your love and the significance of what you have lost. Whether the loss stems from the end of a romantic relationship, the passing of a loved one, or a significant life change, the grieving process is an essential part of healing.

The Nature of Grief

Grief is multifaceted and can manifest in various ways. It is often characterized by an array of emotions, including sadness, anger, confusion, guilt, and sometimes even relief. These emotions can be overwhelming and may come in waves, unexpectedly surfacing at different times and in different intensities.

Understanding that grief is not a linear process is vital. There is no set timeline or right way to grieve. Some days you may feel relatively at peace, while others may plunge you back into deep sorrow. This ebb and flow are natural, and recognizing this can help you navigate the tumultuous journey of grief with greater compassion for yourself.

Why Grieving Matters

Grieving serves several important functions. Firstly, it allows you to process the reality of the loss. Coming to terms with what has happened is a gradual process, and grieving helps your mind and heart to adjust. Secondly, grief provides an outlet for expressing the myriad emotions tied to your loss. Bottling up these feelings can lead to long-term emotional and physical health issues. Finally, grieving honors the significance of your loss. It is a way of acknowledging the impact that person or experience had on your life.

Practical Steps to Allow Yourself to

Grieve

1. Give Yourself Permission:

One of the first steps is simply allowing yourself to grieve. Society often pressures us to "get over it" quickly, but healing cannot be rushed. Understand that it's okay to take your time and that your grief is valid.

2. Embrace Your Emotions:

Allow yourself to feel whatever comes up. Cry when you need to cry, scream if you need to scream, and seek comfort when you need it. There is no "wrong" emotion in grief. Each feeling is a part of the healing process.

3. Create a Ritual:

Establishing a personal ritual can help you honor your loss. This could be lighting a candle, writing a letter to your lost loved one or partner, creating a memory book, or even planting a tree. Rituals provide a sense of closure and a way to pay tribute to what you have lost.

4. Find Healthy Outlets:

Channel your grief into activities that can help you process your emotions. This might include writing, painting, playing music, or engaging in physical activities like running or yoga. Creative and physical outlets can be therapeutic and provide relief from intense emotions.

5. Seek Support:

Reach out to friends, family, or support groups. Talking about your feelings with others who understand can provide immense comfort. Sometimes just knowing that someone else acknowledges your pain can make a significant difference.

6. Be Patient with Yourself:

Grieving is not something you can rush or force. Be patient with yourself and your process. There will be days when you feel like you're making progress and others when it feels like you're back at square one. This is all part of the journey.

The Transformative Power of Grief

While grieving can be excruciating, it also has the potential to be transformative. Through grief, you can discover inner strengths and resilience you never knew you had. The process of grieving can lead to profound personal growth, as it forces you to confront deep emotions and, ultimately, to heal from them.

As you allow yourself to grieve, you

may find that you gain a deeper understanding of yourself and your needs. You might learn to set healthier boundaries, appreciate the value of your emotions, and develop a greater capacity for empathy and compassion toward others who are also suffering.

Remember, grief is not something to be "fixed" or "overcome." It is a journey that needs to be experienced. By allowing yourself to grieve, you are taking an essential step in the healing process. You are honoring your pain and your loss, and in doing so, you are paving the way for healing and eventual acceptance.

Grieving is a powerful testament to the love and connection you shared. It signifies that something meaningful has ended, but it also opens the door to new beginnings and possibilities. Embrace your grief as a natural part of your healing journey, and trust that, over time, you will find your way through the pain to a place of peace and renewal.

- ## Common Emotional Responses

Heartbreak triggers a whirlwind of emotions that can leave you feeling disoriented and overwhelmed. Understanding and identifying these common emotional responses can help you navigate the tumultuous waters of your healing journey with greater clarity and self-compassion. Here, we explore the emotional landscape that often accompanies a broken heart.

1. Sadness and Despair

Sadness is perhaps the most immediate and palpable response to heartbreak. It can feel like a heavy weight pressing down on your chest, making everyday activities seem daunting. This profound sadness stems from the loss of a significant relationship or the future you envisioned. Despair may follow, characterized by a deep sense of hopelessness about the future and a belief that you may never feel happy again.

2. Anger and Resentment

Anger is a natural reaction to feeling hurt and betrayed. You might feel anger toward your ex-partner, yourself, or even the circumstances that led to the heartbreak. This anger can manifest as resentment, fueling thoughts of "how could they do this to me?" or "why didn't I see this coming?"

While these feelings are intense, they are part of the grieving process and serve as a release for the pent-up energy associated with the pain.

3. Shock and Disbelief

The initial shock of a breakup or loss can leave you feeling numb and disoriented. Disbelief sets in as your mind struggles to accept the reality of the situation. You might find yourself replaying events in your head, searching for signs you might have missed or reasons behind the breakup. This state of shock can make it difficult to process your emotions fully, but it is a temporary phase that will eventually give way to more tangible feelings.

4. Guilt and Regret

In the aftermath of heartbreak, it's common to replay the relationship in your mind, scrutinizing your actions and decisions. This can lead to feelings of guilt and regret, where you blame yourself for what went wrong. Thoughts like "If only I had done this differently" or "I should have seen the signs" are pervasive. While self-reflection can be constructive, it's important to remember that relationships are complex, and both parties contribute to their dynamics.

5. Fear and Anxiety

Heartbreak often brings a sense of fear about the future. Questions like "Will I ever find love again?" or "Am I destined to be alone?" can trigger anxiety. This fear is rooted in the uncertainty that follows a significant loss. Additionally, the thought of moving on and opening yourself up to potential future pain can be daunting. Anxiety about starting over and redefining your life without the other person is a natural but challenging aspect of the healing process.

6. Loneliness and Isolation

The end of a relationship can leave a void in your life, leading to feelings of profound loneliness. Activities you once enjoyed together may now seem empty, and the absence of your partner's presence can make you feel isolated. This loneliness is a powerful reminder of the connection you once had, and it can be exacerbated by withdrawing from social interactions. However, recognizing and addressing this loneliness is crucial for your healing.

7. Confusion and Self-Doubt

Heartbreak can shatter your sense of self and leave you questioning your worth and identity. You might feel confused about who you are without the relationship and what you want moving forward. Self-doubt can creep in, causing you to question your attractiveness, intelligence, or likability. It's essential to remind yourself that these feelings are temporary and do not define your true worth.

8. Relief and Liberation

In some cases, heartbreak can bring an unexpected sense of relief. If the relationship was fraught with conflict or unhappiness, its end might free you from ongoing stress and emotional turmoil. This feeling of liberation can be confusing, as it might coexist with sadness and loss. Acknowledging these mixed emotions is important, as it reflects the complexity of your experience.

Navigating These Emotions

Understanding that these emotional responses are a normal part of the healing process can help you navigate them more effectively. Here are some strategies to cope with these intense emotions:

- Allow Yourself to Feel: Suppressing your emotions can

prolong your suffering. Give yourself permission to experience each emotion fully, knowing that it's a necessary part of healing.

- Seek Support: Talk to friends, family, or a therapist about what you're feeling. Sharing your emotions can provide relief and offer new perspectives.

- Practice Self-Compassion: Be gentle with yourself. Recognize that healing takes time and that it's okay to have bad days.

- Stay Active: Engage in activities

that bring you joy or a sense of accomplishment. Physical exercise, hobbies, and socializing can help lift your spirits.

- Reflect and Learn:Use this time to reflect on what you've learned from the relationship and how you can grow from the experience.

Remember, while the journey through heartbreak is painful, it is also a path to greater self-awareness and resilience. By acknowledging and understanding your emotional responses, you take crucial steps toward healing and eventual renewal.

Chapter 2

Self-Care and Healing

• Establishing a Self-Care Routine

After experiencing heartbreak, the journey towards healing can feel overwhelming and uncertain. Establishing a self-care routine is a powerful way to regain control, nurture your well-being, and rebuild your strength. A thoughtfully crafted self-care routine serves as a lifeline, guiding you through the tumultuous waves of emotions and helping you emerge stronger and more resilient.

Understanding the Essence of Self-Care

Self-care is not a luxury or an act of indulgence; it is a fundamental aspect of maintaining physical, emotional, and mental health. It encompasses any activity that we do deliberately to take care of our mental, emotional, and physical health. Especially during times of emotional distress, such as after a breakup, self-care becomes a vital tool for recovery. It allows you to replenish your resources, face challenges with renewed vigor, and foster a sense of normalcy in your life.

The Significance of a Self-Care Routine

Creating a self-care routine is paramount for several reasons:

1. Emotional Healing:

A structured self-care routine provides consistent support and stability, helping you process and release pent-up emotions in a healthy manner.

2. Physical Health:

Regular self-care activities like exercise, proper nutrition, and adequate sleep boost your physical health, which in turn positively impacts your emotional and mental well-being.

3. Mental Clarity:

Engaging in self-care practices helps clear your mind, reduce stress, and enhance focus, making it easier to navigate through your daily life.

4. Rebuilding Identity:

By incorporating activities you love into your routine, you reconnect with your passions and interests, which can help you rediscover your sense of self.

Key Components of a Self-Care Routine

- **Physical Self-Care**

1. Exercise:

Physical activity is a proven way to enhance mood and reduce stress. Exercise releases endorphins, the body's natural feel-good hormones. Whether it's a brisk walk, a yoga session, or a dance class, find an activity that you enjoy and aim to include it in your routine regularly. The goal is to get at least 30 minutes of moderate exercise most days of the week.

2. Nutrition:

A balanced diet is crucial for maintaining energy levels and supporting emotional well-being. Focus on eating a variety of fruits, vegetables, lean proteins, and whole grains. Try to minimize the intake of processed foods, sugar, and caffeine, as these can contribute to mood swings and anxiety. Consider cooking meals at home, experimenting with new recipes, and enjoying the process of preparing nutritious food.

3. Sleep:

Adequate sleep is essential for emotional regulation and mental clarity. Establishing a consistent sleep routine can improve both the quality and quantity of your sleep. Create a relaxing bedtime ritual that may include activities such as reading, meditating, or taking a warm bath. Aim for 7-9 hours of sleep per night and try to wake up and go to bed at the same time each day.

4. Hydration:

Proper hydration is often overlooked but is vital for overall health. Dehydration can affect your mood, energy levels, and cognitive function.

Make it a habit to drink at least eight glasses of water a day. Carry a water bottle with you to ensure you stay hydrated throughout the day.

- **Emotional Self-Care**

1. Journaling:

Writing is a therapeutic way to process your thoughts and emotions. Journaling allows you to explore your feelings, gain insights into your experiences, and track your progress over time. Dedicate a few minutes each day to write about your day, your emotions, and any reflections you have. This practice can provide a sense of release and clarity.

2. Therapy:

Seeking professional help can be incredibly beneficial in navigating the complexities of heartbreak. A therapist can offer guidance, support, and strategies for coping with your emotions. Therapy provides a safe space to discuss your feelings and develop healthier ways to deal with them.

3. Mindfulness and Meditation:

Mindfulness involves staying present in the moment and accepting it without judgment. Meditation is a practice that can enhance mindfulness, reduce stress, and increase emotional stability. Incorporate mindfulness practices such as deep breathing exercises, guided meditations, or simply taking a few minutes each day to sit quietly and observe your thoughts and surroundings.

4. Creative Outlets:

Engaging in creative activities can be a powerful way to express and process emotions. Whether it's painting, drawing, writing poetry, or playing a musical instrument, find a creative outlet that resonates with you. These activities can provide a sense of accomplishment and joy, helping to lift your spirits.

- **Social Self-Care**

1. Support System:

Surround yourself with supportive friends and family who understand what you're going through. Spend time with loved ones who can offer comfort, perspective, and encouragement. Don't hesitate to lean on your support system when you need it.

2. Boundaries:

It's essential to set boundaries with people who may not support your healing process or who bring negativity into your life. This might mean limiting contact with certain individuals or taking a break from social media. Protecting your emotional well-being is a priority.

3. Social Activities:

Engage in social activities that bring you joy and foster a sense of connection. Join a book club, attend a fitness class, or participate in community events. These activities can reduce feelings of isolation and provide opportunities to meet new people and form positive relationships.

- **Spiritual Self-Care**

1. Meditation and Prayer:

If you have a spiritual or religious practice, spending time in meditation or prayer can provide solace and a sense of connection to something greater than yourself. These practices can offer comfort and guidance during challenging times.

2. Nature:

Spending time in nature can be incredibly grounding and healing. Activities like hiking, gardening, or simply walking in a park can foster a sense of peace and renewal. Nature has a way of calming the mind and rejuvenating the spirit.

3. Reflection:

Reflecting on your values, beliefs, and what brings you meaning can help you realign with your sense of purpose. This reflection can be done through journaling, quiet contemplation, or discussions with a trusted mentor or spiritual advisor. Understanding what truly matters to you can provide direction and motivation for your healing journey.

Creating Your Self-Care Routine

Establishing a self-care routine

involves identifying activities that nourish your body, mind, and spirit and incorporating them into your daily life. Here are some steps to help you create a personalized self-care routine:

1. Assess Your Needs:

Reflect on the areas of your life that need the most attention. Consider your physical health, emotional well-being, social connections, and spiritual needs. Identify activities that address these areas.

2. Set Realistic Goals:

Start with small, achievable goals. For example, aim to exercise three times a week, journal for ten minutes each day, or spend 15 minutes in meditation. Gradually increase the time and frequency of these activities as they become habits.

3. Create a Schedule:

Integrate self-care activities into your daily or weekly schedule. Treat these activities as non-negotiable appointments with yourself. Consistency is key to establishing and maintaining a self-care routine.

4. Stay Flexible:

Life can be unpredictable, so it's important to remain flexible with your self-care routine. If you miss a day or need to adjust your schedule, don't be too hard on yourself. The goal is to prioritize your well-being, not to add more stress.

5. Evaluate and Adjust:

Regularly assess how your self-care routine is working for you. Are the activities you've chosen helping you feel better? Are there areas that need more attention? Adjust your routine as needed to ensure it continues to meet your needs.

Embracing Self-Care as a Lifelong Practice

Self-care is not just a temporary solution for healing after heartbreak; it is a lifelong practice that supports overall well-being. By establishing a self-care routine now, you are laying the foundation for a healthier, more balanced life. Embrace self-care as an essential part of your daily routine, and remember that taking care of yourself is a vital step towards healing and finding happiness again.

Establishing a self-care routine is a powerful act of self-love and a crucial step in healing a broken heart. By prioritizing your physical, emotional, and spiritual well-being, you create a supportive environment for yourself to heal, grow, and thrive. Remember, self-care is not selfish—it is necessary. As you navigate the journey of heartbreak, let self-care be your guide, helping you rediscover your strength, resilience, and capacity for joy.

• The Role of Physical Health in Emotional Healing

Heartbreak is one of the most challenging experiences one can endure. The emotional turmoil it brings can be overwhelming, affecting various aspects of your life, including your physical health. However, physical health plays a crucial role in emotional healing, and understanding this connection can significantly enhance your recovery journey. In this chapter, we will explore how physical health influences emotional well-being, the impact of different physical activities, and practical steps to integrate physical health into your emotional healing process.

Understanding the Mind-Body Connection

The mind-body connection is a fundamental concept that highlights the interdependence of physical and emotional health. When we experience emotional distress, our bodies respond in various ways, often manifesting symptoms such as fatigue, headaches, muscle tension, and changes in appetite. Conversely, maintaining good physical health can positively impact our mental and emotional state.

How Physical Health Influences Emotional Healing

1. Hormonal Balance:

Physical activities stimulate the release of endorphins, dopamine, serotonin, and oxytocin—chemicals in the brain that promote feelings of happiness, reduce stress, and enhance overall mood. These hormones act as natural painkillers and mood elevators, helping to mitigate the feelings of sadness and anxiety often associated with heartbreak.

2. Stress Reduction:

Exercise reduces the levels of stress hormones such as adrenaline and cortisol. High levels of these hormones can lead to increased feelings of stress and anxiety. Regular physical activity helps to balance these hormone levels, promoting a sense of calm and relaxation.

3. Improved Sleep:

Physical health is closely linked to sleep quality. Regular exercise can help regulate sleep patterns, leading to deeper and more restful sleep. Quality sleep is essential for emotional resilience, cognitive function, and overall mental health. It allows the brain to process emotions, consolidate memories, and rejuvenate.

4. Increased Energy Levels:

Engaging in physical activity boosts your energy levels by improving cardiovascular health, enhancing oxygen circulation, and increasing overall stamina. Higher energy levels can lead to a more positive outlook on life and a greater ability to engage in daily activities, including those that bring joy and fulfillment.

5. Enhanced Cognitive Function:

Exercise has been shown to improve cognitive functions such as memory, attention, and problem-solving skills. These improvements can help you think more clearly, make better decisions, and maintain focus, which are crucial for navigating the complexities of emotional healing.

6. Boosted Immune System: Maintaining good physical health strengthens the immune system, reducing the likelihood of illness and enhancing overall well-being. A strong immune system helps you stay physically healthy, which is vital for supporting emotional health during challenging times.

The Impact of Different Physical Activities

Different types of physical activities offer unique benefits for emotional healing. Here, we will explore several activities and how they can contribute to your emotional well-being.

1. Aerobic Exercise:

Activities such as running, swimming, cycling, and dancing elevate your heart rate and increase the release of endorphins. These exercises are particularly effective at reducing symptoms of depression and anxiety. They also improve cardiovascular health, which is essential for overall vitality and energy.

2. Strength Training:

Lifting weights, doing bodyweight exercises, or using resistance bands can help build muscle strength and endurance. Strength training not only improves physical health but also enhances self-esteem and body image, which can be particularly beneficial after a breakup.

3. Yoga*:

Yoga combines physical postures, breathing exercises, and meditation. It is excellent for reducing stress, improving flexibility, and promoting relaxation. Yoga encourages mindfulness, helping you stay present and centered, which is crucial for processing emotions and reducing anxiety.

4. Pilates:

Similar to yoga, Pilates focuses on core strength, flexibility, and overall body awareness. It can improve posture, reduce back pain, and enhance mental clarity. The mindful movements and breath control in Pilates can also aid in reducing stress and promoting emotional balance.

5. Walking and Hiking:

Walking, especially in nature, can have profound effects on emotional health. It offers a gentle way to get moving, clear your mind, and connect with your surroundings. Hiking, in particular, can provide a sense of adventure and accomplishment, boosting your mood and self-confidence.

6. Team Sports and Group Activities:

Participating in team sports or group fitness classes can offer social support, camaraderie, and a sense of community. These activities help combat feelings of loneliness and isolation, providing a fun and engaging way to stay active.

7. Dancing:

Dancing is a joyful and expressive form of exercise. It allows you to release pent-up emotions, connect with music, and enjoy the company of others if done in a group setting.

Dancing can significantly elevate your mood and provide a sense of freedom and creativity.

Practical Steps to Integrate Physical Health into Emotional Healing

1. Set Realistic Goals:

Start by setting achievable fitness goals that align with your current physical condition and emotional state. Gradually increase the intensity and duration of your workouts as you build strength and confidence. Setting and achieving small goals can provide a sense of accomplishment and motivation.

2. Create a Routine:

Establishing a consistent exercise routine can provide structure and stability during a time of emotional upheaval. Schedule regular workout sessions, whether it's a morning jog, a lunchtime yoga class, or an evening walk. Consistency is key to reaping the long-term benefits of physical activity.

3. Listen to Your Body:

Pay attention to how your body feels during and after exercise. It's essential to push yourself enough to gain the benefits of physical activity, but not to the point of injury or burnout. Rest when needed and be gentle with yourself, especially on emotionally challenging days.

4. Combine Activities:

Mix different types of exercises to keep your routine interesting and comprehensive. For example, combine aerobic exercises with strength training, yoga, and recreational activities. Variety can prevent boredom and ensure you engage different muscle groups and aspects of fitness.

5. Find Joy in Movement:

Choose activities that you genuinely

enjoy. Whether it's dancing, hiking, swimming, or playing a sport, engaging in enjoyable physical activities can make exercise feel less like a chore and more like a source of pleasure and stress relief.

6. Social Support:

Exercise with friends, join fitness classes, or participate in group activities to build a support network. Social connections can provide encouragement, accountability, and a sense of community, which are crucial for emotional healing.

7. Mind-Body Practices:

Incorporate mind-body exercises like yoga, tai chi, or Pilates into your routine. These practices not only improve physical health but also enhance mental clarity, reduce stress, and promote emotional balance.

8. Track Your Progress:

Keep a journal or use a fitness app to track your physical activity, progress, and how you feel after workouts. Reflecting on your achievements and noticing improvements in your mood and energy levels can boost motivation and reinforce the positive impact of exercise.

9. Reward Yourself:

Celebrate your progress by rewarding yourself with something enjoyable, such as a relaxing bath, a massage, or a favorite healthy treat. Recognizing your efforts and achievements can enhance your sense of accomplishment and motivate you to continue.

10. Stay Patient and Compassionate:

Healing is a gradual process, and it's essential to be patient with yourself. There will be days when you feel more motivated and days when you struggle. Embrace the journey with compassion and acknowledge that every step forward, no matter how small, is a victory.

Integrating Physical Health with Other Self-Care Practices

Physical health is a crucial component of emotional healing, but it works best when integrated with other self-care practices. Combine physical activity with healthy eating, adequate sleep, mindfulness practices, and social connections for a holistic approach to healing. This comprehensive strategy can create a strong foundation for emotional resilience and overall well-being.

The role of physical health in emotional healing cannot be overstated. By prioritizing physical activity and incorporating it into your self-care routine, you can significantly enhance your emotional recovery and overall well-being. The journey through heartbreak is undoubtedly challenging, but by nurturing your body and mind through regular exercise, balanced nutrition, and mindful practices, you pave the way for a healthier, happier, and more resilient self. Embrace the power of physical health as a vital ally in your healing journey and allow it to guide you towards a brighter and more fulfilling future.

• **Mindfulness and Meditation Techniques**

Heartbreak is an emotionally overwhelming experience that can affect every aspect of your life. When dealing with the aftermath of a broken heart, finding inner peace and stability becomes crucial. Mindfulness and meditation are powerful tools that can help you navigate this difficult period with grace and resilience. In this chapter, we will explore various mindfulness and meditation techniques that can aid in healing a broken heart, providing practical steps and insights to integrate these practices into your daily life.

Understanding Mindfulness and Meditation

- **What is Mindfulness?**

Mindfulness is the practice of being fully present and engaged in the current moment, aware of your thoughts, feelings, and sensations without judgment. It involves paying attention to the here and now, rather than getting lost in past regrets or future worries. Mindfulness helps you develop a deeper understanding of your emotions and thoughts, fostering a sense of calm and clarity.

- **What is Meditation?**

Meditation is a practice that involves focusing the mind and eliminating distractions to achieve a state of mental clarity and emotional calm. It often involves techniques such as deep breathing, visualization, or the repetition of a mantra. Meditation helps you cultivate a sense of inner peace and balance, making it an invaluable tool for emotional healing.

The Benefits of Mindfulness and

Meditation

1. Reduces Stress and Anxiety:

Mindfulness and meditation lower levels of cortisol, the stress hormone, helping to alleviate anxiety and tension.

2. Improves Emotional Regulation:

These practices enhance your ability to manage and process emotions, reducing emotional reactivity.

3. Enhances Self-Awareness:

By observing your thoughts and feelings without judgment, you gain greater self-awareness and insight into your emotional patterns.

4. Promotes Relaxation:

Meditation induces a state of deep relaxation, which can be particularly soothing during times of emotional distress.

5. Increases Resilience:

Regular practice builds emotional resilience, helping you cope better with challenging situations.

Mindfulness Techniques

1. Mindful Breathing

Mindful breathing is a simple yet effective technique that involves focusing your attention on your breath.

This practice can help anchor you in the present moment and provide a sense of calm.

How to Practice Mindful Breathing:

- Find a Comfortable Position*: Sit or lie down in a comfortable position, with your back straight and shoulders relaxed.

- **Focus on Your Breath**: Close your eyes and take a deep breath in through your nose, allowing your abdomen to expand. Exhale slowly through your mouth.

- Notice the Sensations: Pay

attention to the sensation of the air entering and leaving your body. Notice the rise and fall of your chest or abdomen with each breath.

- Stay Present: If your mind starts to wander, gently bring your focus back to your breath without judgment. Continue this practice for 5-10 minutes or longer if you wish.

2. Body Scan Meditation

Body scan meditation involves paying attention to different parts of your body, from your toes to your head. This technique helps you become more aware of physical sensations and release tension.

How to Practice Body Scan Meditation:

- Find a Quiet Space: Lie down on your back with your arms resting by your sides, palms facing up. Close your eyes.

- Start with Your Toes: Bring your attention to your toes. Notice any sensations—warmth, tingling, tension, or relaxation.

- Move Upward: Gradually move

your focus up through your body, part by part—feet, ankles, calves, knees, thighs, hips, abdomen, chest, back, shoulders, arms, hands, neck, and finally your head.

- Observe Without Judgment: As you scan each part, simply observe any sensations without trying to change them. If you notice tension, imagine it melting away with each breath.

- Complete the Scan: Once you reach the top of your head, take a few deep breaths and gently bring your awareness back to the present moment.

3. Mindful Walking

Mindful walking involves paying close attention to the experience of walking, using it as an opportunity to practice mindfulness.

How to Practice Mindful Walking:

- Choose a Path: Find a quiet place where you can walk undisturbed. It can be indoors or outdoors.

- Focus on Your Steps: Start walking slowly, paying attention to the sensation of your feet touching the ground. Notice the movement of your legs and the shift in your weight.

- Engage Your Senses: Observe your surroundings using all your senses. Notice the sights, sounds, smells, and even the feeling of the air on your skin.

- Stay Present: If your mind starts to wander, gently bring your focus back to the act of walking. Continue for 10-20 minutes, or as long as you feel comfortable.

4. Mindful Eating

Mindful eating involves paying full attention to the experience of eating, savoring each bite, and being aware of the sensations and emotions associated with eating.

How to Practice Mindful Eating:

- Choose a Meal or Snack: Select a meal or snack that you enjoy and can eat without distractions.

- Observe Your Food: Before you start eating, take a moment to look at your food. Notice the colors, textures, and aromas.

- Take Small Bites: Eat slowly, taking small bites. Chew

thoroughly and pay attention to the flavors and textures in your mouth.

- Stay Present: Focus on the act of eating. Notice how your body feels as you eat—how the food tastes, the sensations in your mouth, and how your stomach feels as it fills.

- Express Gratitude: Take a moment to express gratitude for the food you are eating and for the nourishment it provides.

5. Mindful Listening

Mindful listening involves fully

focusing on the sounds around you or on a piece of music, without judgment or distraction.

How to Practice Mindful Listening:

- Find a Quiet Space: Sit comfortably in a quiet space or put on a piece of music you enjoy.

- Focus on the Sounds: Close your eyes and focus on the sounds around you. If you are listening to music, pay attention to the different instruments, melodies, and rhythms.

- Stay Present: If your mind starts

to wander, gently bring your focus back to the sounds. Allow yourself to fully immerse in the auditory experience.

- Observe Your Emotions: Notice any emotions or thoughts that arise as you listen. Simply observe them without judgment.

Meditation Techniques

1. Guided Meditation

Guided meditation involves listening to a narrator who guides you through a meditation session. This technique is particularly helpful for beginners.

How to Practice Guided Meditation:

- Find a Comfortable Position: Sit or lie down in a comfortable position.

- Choose a Guided Meditation: Select a guided meditation that resonates with you. There are many options available online or through meditation apps.

- Listen and Follow: Close your eyes and listen to the narrator's instructions. Follow their guidance, allowing yourself to fully engage with the meditation.

- Reflect: After the session, take a few moments to reflect on your experience and how you feel.

2. Loving-Kindness Meditation

Loving-kindness meditation, also known as Metta meditation, focuses on cultivating feelings of love and compassion towards yourself and others.

How to Practice Loving-Kindness Meditation:

- Find a Quiet Space: Sit comfortably in a quiet space.

- Focus on Your Breath: Close your eyes and take a few deep breaths to center yourself.

- Repeat Affirmations: Silently repeat phrases such as "May I be happy, may I be healthy, may I be safe, may I live with ease." Feel the emotions these words evoke.

- Extend to Others: Gradually extend these wishes to others, starting with loved ones, then acquaintances, and finally all beings. For example, "May you be happy, may you be healthy, may you be safe, may you live with ease."

- Reflect: Take a moment to reflect on the feelings of love and compassion that arose during the meditation.

3. Visualization Meditation

Visualization meditation involves imagining a peaceful scene or a positive outcome, helping to create a sense of calm and positivity.

How to Practice Visualization Meditation:

- Find a Comfortable Position: Sit or lie down in a comfortable position.

- Focus on Your Breath: Close your eyes and take a few deep breaths to relax.

- Create a Mental Image: Visualize a peaceful place, such as a beach, forest, or mountain. Imagine all the details—the sights, sounds, smells, and sensations.

- Immerse Yourself: Immerse yourself in the scene, allowing it to bring you a sense of peace and relaxation.

- Positive Outcome Visualization: Alternatively, you can visualize a positive outcome for a specific situation. Imagine it in detail and feel the emotions associated with that outcome.

- Reflect: After the meditation, take a few moments to reflect on the experience and how it made you feel.

4. Mantra Meditation

Mantra meditation involves repeating a word or phrase to help focus the mind and induce a state of calm.

How to Practice Mantra Meditation:

- Choose a Mantra: Select a word or phrase that resonates with you, such as "peace," "love," or "I am calm."

- Find a Comfortable Position: Sit or lie down in a comfortable position.

- Focus on Your Breath: Close your eyes and take a few deep breaths to relax.

- Repeat the Mantra: Silently repeat your chosen mantra with each inhale and exhale. Focus on the sound and vibration of the words.

- Stay Present: If your mind wanders, gently bring your attention back to the mantra. Allow the repetition to help quiet your thoughts and bring you into a state of calm.

- Reflect: After the meditation, take a few moments to reflect on how you feel and the impact of the mantra on your state of mind.

5. Mindfulness Meditation

Mindfulness meditation involves observing your thoughts, emotions, and sensations without judgment. This practice helps you develop a deeper awareness of your internal experience.

How to Practice Mindfulness Meditation:

- Find a Quiet Space: Sit

comfortably in a quiet space.

- Focus on Your Breath: Close your eyes and take a few deep breaths to center yourself.

- Observe Your Thoughts: Allow your thoughts to flow naturally without trying to control or judge them. Simply observe them as they come and go.

- Notice Your Emotions: Pay attention to any emotions that arise. Acknowledge them without judgment and notice how they affect your body and mind.

- Scan Your Body: Do a quick body scan, noticing any physical sensations. Observe areas of tension or relaxation.

- Return to the Breath: If you find yourself getting caught up in thoughts or emotions, gently bring your focus back to your breath. Continue this practice for 10-20 minutes or longer if you wish.

- Reflect: After the meditation, take a few moments to reflect on your experience and any insights or feelings that arose.

Integrating Mindfulness and Meditation into Daily Life

• Creating a Consistent Practice

1. Set Aside Time:

Dedicate a specific time each day for your mindfulness and meditation practice. This could be in the morning to start your day with calm or in the evening to wind down.

2. Start Small:

Begin with short sessions, such as 5-10 minutes, and gradually increase the duration as you become more comfortable with the practice.

3. Be Patient:

Developing a consistent practice takes time and patience. Be gentle with yourself and allow the practice to evolve naturally.

- **Incorporating Mindfulness into Everyday Activities**

1. Mindful Eating:

Practice mindful eating during meals by paying full attention to the taste, texture, and aroma of your food. Chew slowly and savor each bite.

2. Mindful Walking:

Incorporate mindful walking into your daily routine. Pay attention to the sensation of your feet touching the ground, the movement of your body, and the sights and sounds around you.

3. Mindful Listening:

Practice mindful listening during conversations. Fully engage with the person speaking, without planning your response or getting distracted by other thoughts.

4. Mindful Cleaning:

Turn household chores into a mindfulness practice. Focus on the sensations of cleaning, such as the feel of the cloth in your hand or the smell of cleaning products.

5. Mindful Breathing:

Take short mindfulness breaks throughout the day by focusing on your breath for a few minutes. This can help you stay grounded and reduce stress.

- **Using Technology to Support Your Practice**

1. Meditation Apps:

Utilize meditation apps that offer guided meditations, timers, and tracking features to support your practice. Popular apps include Headspace, Calm, and Insight Timer.

2. Online Resources:

Explore online resources such as videos, articles, and courses that provide instruction and inspiration for mindfulness and meditation.

3. Community Groups:

Join online or local meditation groups to connect with others and share your experiences. Community support can enhance your practice and provide motivation.

Overcoming Challenges in

Mindfulness and Meditation

• Dealing with Distractions

1. Acknowledge the Distraction:

When you notice a distraction, acknowledge it without judgment and gently bring your focus back to your breath or the present moment.

2. Create a Quiet Environment:

Minimize external distractions by creating a quiet, comfortable space for your practice. This can help you stay focused and reduce interruptions.

3. Be Kind to Yourself: Understand that distractions are a natural part of the

practice. Be kind to yourself and view each distraction as an opportunity to strengthen your focus.

- **Managing Difficult Emotions**

1. Observe Without Judgment:

When difficult emotions arise, observe them without judgment. Acknowledge their presence and allow yourself to feel them fully.

2. Practice Self-Compassion:

Offer yourself compassion and understanding during challenging times. Remind yourself that it is okay to experience difficult emotions and that they are a natural part of the healing process.

3. Seek Support:

If you find certain emotions overwhelming, seek support from a trusted friend, therapist, or support group. Sharing your feelings can provide relief and help you process your emotions.

- **Staying Consistent**

1. Set Realistic Goals:

Set realistic goals for your mindfulness and meditation practice. Start with small, achievable goals and gradually increase them as you become more comfortable.

2. Create a Routine:

Establish a daily routine that includes your practice. Consistency is key to reaping the benefits of mindfulness and meditation.

3. Track Your Progress:

Keep a journal or use an app to track your progress. Reflecting on your journey can help you stay motivated and committed to your practice.

Mindfulness and meditation are invaluable tools for healing a broken heart. By cultivating a regular practice, you can develop greater self-awareness, emotional regulation, and inner peace. These practices offer a sanctuary of calm and clarity, helping you navigate the complexities of heartbreak with grace and resilience. Embrace mindfulness and meditation as essential components of your healing journey, and allow them to guide you towards a place of acceptance, understanding, and emotional well-being.

Chapter 3

Rebuilding Self-Esteem

• Identifying Negative Self -Talk

Heartbreak is a painful experience that can leave you feeling vulnerable, lost, and overwhelmed. During this time, the way you talk to yourself can significantly impact your emotional recovery. Negative self-talk, or the critical and often harsh inner dialogue, can exacerbate feelings of sadness, anxiety, and low self-esteem, making it even more challenging to heal. Identifying and addressing negative self-talk is a crucial step in the journey to emotional recovery. In this chapter, we will explore the nature of negative self-talk, its impact on your mental health, and strategies to identify and transform it into a more compassionate and supportive inner dialogue.

Understanding Negative Self-Talk

- **What is Negative Self-Talk?**

Negative self-talk refers to the critical

and often irrational thoughts you have about yourself. It can take many forms, such as blaming yourself for the breakup, doubting your worth, or predicting a bleak future. These thoughts are usually automatic and can become a deeply ingrained habit over time.

- **Types of Negative Self-Talk**

1. Catastrophizing:

Expecting the worst-case scenario to happen. For example, "I'll never find love again" or "My life is ruined."

2. Personalizing:

Blaming yourself for events beyond

your control. For example, "The breakup is all my fault" or "I should have done things differently."

3. Overgeneralizing:

Making broad, negative conclusions based on a single event. For example, "I'll always be alone" or "Relationships never work out for me."

4. Black-and-White Thinking:

Seeing things in extremes, with no middle ground. For example, "I'm either a complete success or a total failure" or "If I'm not perfect, I'm worthless."

5. Filtering:

Focusing only on the negative aspects of a situation, while ignoring the positive. For example, "I only remember the fights" or "None of the good times matter now."

6. Labeling:

Attaching negative labels to yourself or others. For example, "I'm a loser" or "They're a heartbreaker."

- **The Impact of Negative Self-Talk**

Negative self-talk can have a profound impact on your mental and emotional well-being. It can:

1. Lower Self-Esteem:

Constant self-criticism can erode your self-esteem, making you feel unworthy and undeserving of love and happiness.

2. Increase Anxiety and Depression:

Negative thoughts can fuel feelings of anxiety and depression, creating a cycle of negativity that is hard to break.

3. Hinder Healing:

Dwelling on negative thoughts can prevent you from moving forward and finding closure, prolonging the healing process.

4. Affect Physical Health:

Chronic stress and negative thinking can take a toll on your physical health, leading to issues such as fatigue, headaches, and weakened immune function.

5. Impact Relationships:

Negative self-talk can affect your interactions with others, making it difficult to form and maintain healthy relationships.

Identifying Negative Self-Talk

- **Becoming Aware of Your Inner Dialogue**

The first step in addressing negative self-talk is becoming aware of it. Many people are so accustomed to their inner critic that they don't even realize it's there. Here are some strategies to help you become more aware of your negative self-talk:

1. Mindfulness:

Practice mindfulness to become more present and aware of your thoughts. Notice when negative thoughts arise and observe them without judgment.

2. Journaling:

Write down your thoughts and feelings regularly. Reviewing your journal entries can help you identify patterns of negative thinking.

3. Self-Reflection:

Take time to reflect on your inner dialogue. Ask yourself questions like, "What am I thinking right now?" and "Is this thought helpful or harmful?"

4. Check Your Emotions:

Pay attention to your emotions. Negative feelings such as sadness, anger, or anxiety can be indicators of negative self-talk.

- **Common Triggers of Negative Self-Talk**

Identifying the triggers of your

negative self-talk can help you address the root causes. Common triggers include:

1. Breakup-Related Events:

Reminders of your ex-partner, such as seeing their belongings or visiting places you used to go together.

2. Stressful Situations:

High-stress situations can amplify negative self-talk, making you more critical of yourself.

3. Comparisons:

Comparing yourself to others, especially on social media, can trigger negative thoughts about your worth and achievements.

4. Past Trauma:

Previous experiences of rejection, failure, or trauma can resurface and fuel negative self-talk during heartbreak.

5. Perfectionism:

Holding yourself to unrealistic standards can lead to constant self-criticism and feelings of inadequacy.

- **Techniques for Identifying Negative Self-Talk**

1. Thought Monitoring:

Keep track of your thoughts throughout the day. When you notice a negative thought, write it down. Over time, you will begin to see patterns in your thinking.

2. Thought Journaling:

Use a dedicated journal to record your thoughts and feelings. Include details about what triggered the thought, how it made you feel, and how you responded to it.

3. Cognitive Behavioral Therapy (CBT) Techniques:

CBT techniques, such as thought records and cognitive restructuring, can help you identify and challenge negative thoughts. These techniques involve examining the evidence for and against your thoughts and developing more balanced perspectives.

4. Mindfulness Meditation:

Regular mindfulness meditation can increase your awareness of your thoughts and help you recognize when you are engaging in negative self-talk.

Transforming Negative Self-Talk

- **Challenging Negative Thoughts**

Once you have identified your negative self-talk, the next step is to challenge and reframe these thoughts. Here are some strategies to help you do this:

1. Examine the Evidence:

Ask yourself if there is factual evidence to support your negative thought. Often, negative self-talk is based on irrational beliefs rather than reality.

2. Alternative Explanations:

Consider alternative explanations for the situation. For example, instead of thinking, "I'm unlovable," consider, "This relationship didn't work out, but it doesn't mean I'm unlovable."

3. Perspective Shift:

Try to view the situation from a different perspective. Ask yourself how a compassionate friend might view the situation or what advice you would give to someone else in your position.

4. Positive Affirmations:

Replace negative thoughts with positive affirmations. For example, if you catch yourself thinking, "I'm a failure," replace it with, "I am capable and resilient."

5. Self-Compassion:

Practice self-compassion by treating yourself with the same kindness and understanding you would offer to a friend. Acknowledge your pain and remind yourself that it's okay to feel hurt and to take time to heal.

- **Developing a Positive Inner Dialogue**

Cultivating a positive inner dialogue takes practice, but it can significantly enhance your emotional well-being. Here are some techniques to help you develop a more supportive and compassionate inner voice:

1. Gratitude Practice:

Regularly practice gratitude by reflecting on the positive aspects of your life. This can help shift your focus away from negative thoughts and towards a more positive outlook.

2. Daily Affirmations: Start your day with positive affirmations that reinforce your self-worth and capabilities. Write them down or say them aloud to yourself.

3. Visualization: Visualize yourself overcoming challenges and achieving your goals. This can help build confidence and reduce self-doubt.

4. Surround Yourself with Positivity**: Engage with positive influences, such as supportive friends, uplifting books,

and inspirational content. Surrounding yourself with positivity can reinforce a positive mindset.

5. Practice Self-Care: Prioritize self-care activities that nurture your physical, emotional, and mental well-being. Taking care of yourself can boost your self-esteem and resilience.

Long-Term Strategies for Positive Self-Talk

Developing and maintaining positive self-talk is an ongoing process. Here are some long-term strategies to help you sustain a healthy inner dialogue:

1. Regular Self-Reflection: Set aside

time regularly for self-reflection to check in with your thoughts and emotions. This can help you stay aware of any negative self-talk and address it promptly.

2. Continuous Learning: Educate yourself about mindfulness, self-compassion, and cognitive restructuring techniques. The more tools you have at your disposal, the better equipped you will be to manage negative thoughts.

3. Seek Support: Don't hesitate to seek support from a therapist or counselor if you find it challenging to manage negative self-talk on your own.

Professional support can provide valuable insights and strategies.

4. Celebrate Progress: Acknowledge and celebrate your progress in developing positive self-talk. Recognize the effort you have put into changing your inner dialogue and the positive impact it has had on your life.

5. Stay Committed: Commit to ongoing practice and self-care. Building a positive inner dialogue is a lifelong journey, and staying committed to your mental and emotional well-being is essential.

Identifying and transforming negative

self-talk is a crucial step in healing a broken heart. By becoming aware of your inner dialogue, challenging negative thoughts, and cultivating a more compassionate and supportive inner voice, you can significantly enhance your emotional recovery. Remember that this process takes time and practice, but the effort is well worth it. As you develop a healthier relationship with yourself, you will find greater resilience, self-esteem, and peace, paving the way for a brighter and more fulfilling future. Embrace the journey with patience and kindness, knowing that each step you take brings you closer to healing and wholeness.

• **Cultivating Self-Compassion**

Heartbreak can leave you feeling raw, vulnerable, and harshly critical of yourself. In such times, self-compassion is not just a balm but a vital component of emotional recovery. Cultivating self-compassion involves treating yourself with the same kindness, understanding, and care that you would offer to a close friend. This chapter delves into the importance of self-compassion, how it can transform your healing process, and practical strategies to foster a compassionate relationship with yourself.

Understanding Self-Compassion

Self-compassion is the practice of extending kindness and understanding to yourself, especially in moments of suffering, failure, or perceived inadequacy. It is based on three core components:

1. Self-Kindness: Being warm and understanding toward yourself when you suffer, fail, or feel inadequate, rather than ignoring your pain or self-flagellating with criticism.

2. Common Humanity: Recognizing that suffering and personal inadequacy are part of the shared human experience – something that we all go through rather than something that happens to "me" alone.

3. Mindfulness: Holding your experience in balanced awareness, rather than ignoring your pain or exaggerating it. Mindfulness requires that you do not over-identify with negative thoughts and emotions, thereby allowing you to maintain perspective.

The Benefits of Self-Compassion

1. Improved Emotional Resilience: Self -compassion helps you navigate emotional pain more effectively, reducing the intensity and duration of negative feelings.

2. Enhanced Self-Esteem: By treating yourself kindly, you foster a positive self-view that isn't contingent on external validation or success.

3. Reduced Anxiety and Depression: Self-compassion can diminish symptoms of anxiety and depression by interrupting the cycle of negative self-talk and self-criticism.

4. Better Relationships: When you are

compassionate with yourself, you are more likely to extend the same kindness to others, improving your relationships and fostering deeper connections.

5. Greater Life Satisfaction: Self-compassionate individuals tend to have higher levels of happiness and life satisfaction, as they are more forgiving of their own mistakes and more accepting of their life circumstances.

Recognizing the Need for Self-Compassion

It can be challenging to recognize

when you need to be more self-compassionate, especially if you are accustomed to self-criticism. Here are some signs that you might benefit from cultivating self-compassion:

1. Persistent Self-Criticism: You frequently blame yourself for the breakup or dwell on your perceived flaws and mistakes.

2. Low Self-Esteem: You struggle with feelings of unworthiness and believe that you do not deserve love or happiness.

3. Perfectionism: You set unattainably high standards for yourself and feel

devastated when you fail to meet them.

4. Avoidance of Emotions: You suppress or ignore your emotions, believing that you need to "be strong" and not show vulnerability.

5. Comparison with Others: You constantly compare yourself to others, feeling inferior or envious of their perceived success and happiness.

The Inner Critic

The inner critic is a common obstacle to self-compassion. This internal voice magnifies your faults, highlights your failures, and undermines your self-worth. Identifying and understanding your inner critic is the first step towards transforming self-criticism into self-compassion.

Common Themes of the Inner Critic:

1. **Blame**: "It's all my fault."

2. **Shame**: "I'm not good enough."

3. **Hopelessness**: "I'll never be happy again."

4. **Fear**: "I'm unlovable and will always be alone."

5. **Regret**: "If only I had done things differently."

Practical Strategies for Cultivating

Self-Compassion

- **Self-Kindness Practices**

1. Positive Self-Talk: Replace self-critical thoughts with compassionate, supportive ones. For example, instead of saying, "I'm such a failure," try saying, "I'm doing the best I can, and that's enough."

2. Self-Soothing: Engage in activities that bring you comfort and joy, such as taking a warm bath, listening to your favorite music, or spending time in nature.

3. Affirmations: Create and repeat positive affirmations that remind you

of your worth and strength. Examples include "I am worthy of love and compassion" and "I am enough just as I am."

- **Practicing Mindfulness**

Mindfulness is a key component of self-compassion, helping you stay present and non-judgmental toward your thoughts and feelings.

1. Mindful Breathing: Focus on your breath to anchor yourself in the present moment. Notice the sensation of the air entering and leaving your body.

2. Body Scan: Perform a body scan to

become aware of physical sensations, tension, and areas of comfort. This practice helps you reconnect with your body and its needs.

3. Mindful Observation: Take a few moments to observe your surroundings with full attention. Notice the colors, shapes, and textures without judgment.

- **Embracing Common Humanity**

Recognizing that suffering is a universal experience can reduce feelings of isolation and self-pity.

1. Shared Experience: Remind yourself that many others have experienced

heartbreak and have gone through similar emotions. You are not alone in your suffering.

2. Connecting with Others: Share your feelings with trusted friends or join support groups where you can hear about others' experiences and offer mutual support.

- **Reframing Negative Thoughts**

Challenging and reframing negative thoughts can help you develop a more compassionate perspective.

1. Identify Negative Thoughts: Write down negative thoughts as they arise. Be specific about the triggers and

emotions associated with them.

2. Examine the Evidence: Look for evidence that contradicts your negative thoughts. Ask yourself if there is a more compassionate and realistic way to view the situation.

3. Create Balanced Statements: Replace negative thoughts with balanced, self-compassionate statements. For example, "I made mistakes, but I am learning and growing from this experience."

- **Self-Compassion Exercises**

1. The Self-Compassion Break: When you are feeling stressed or upset, take

a moment to practice a self-compassion break. Place your hand over your heart, acknowledge your suffering, remind yourself that suffering is part of the human experience, and offer yourself words of kindness.

2. Writing a Compassionate Letter: Write a letter to yourself from the perspective of a compassionate friend. Offer understanding, comfort, and advice as you would to someone you care about deeply.

3. Loving-Kindness Meditation: Practice loving-kindness meditation by silently repeating phrases of goodwill

toward yourself. For example, "May I be happy. May I be healthy. May I be safe. May I live with ease."

Overcoming Obstacles to Self-Compassion

- **Dealing with Resistance**

Cultivating self-compassion can sometimes feel uncomfortable or unnatural, especially if you are used to being self-critical. Here are some common forms of resistance and how to address them:

1. Fear of Self-Indulgence: You may worry that self-compassion is self-

indulgent or will make you complacent. Remember that self-compassion involves caring for yourself in a way that supports your well-being and growth, not avoiding responsibility.

2. Guilt: You might feel guilty about being kind to yourself, especially if you believe you are to blame for the breakup. Understand that everyone makes mistakes, and you deserve kindness and forgiveness just as much as anyone else.

3. Doubt: You may doubt your ability to be self-compassionate or feel that you don't deserve it. Challenge these doubts by reminding yourself of the

inherent worth and dignity of every person, including yourself.

- **Building a Supportive Environment**

Creating an environment that supports your practice of self-compassion can enhance your efforts.

1. Seek Positive Influences: Surround yourself with people who are supportive, understanding, and kind. Distance yourself from those who are critical or unsupportive.

2. Incorporate Self-Compassion into Your Routine: Integrate self-compassion practices into your daily routine. Set aside time each day for mindfulness, affirmations, and self-care activities.

3. Create Reminders: Use visual reminders, such as sticky notes with positive messages or inspirational quotes, to reinforce your commitment to self-compassion.

Long-Term Strategies for Self-Compassion

- **Developing a Self-Compassionate Mindset**

Cultivating a self-compassionate mindset involves ongoing practice and commitment.

1. Regular Practice: Make self-compassion a regular part of your life by incorporating it into your daily routine. Consistency is key to developing a compassionate mindset.

2. Reflect on Progress: Take time to reflect on your progress and celebrate your efforts. Acknowledge the positive changes in your self-talk and emotional well-being.

3. Continuous Learning: Continue learning about self-compassion

through books, workshops, and online resources. The more you understand and practice self-compassion, the more it will become a natural part of your life.

- **Self-Compassion in Challenging Times**

Self-compassion is especially important during difficult times. Here are some strategies to maintain self-compassion when faced with challenges:

1. Practice Patience: Understand that healing is a process that takes time. Be patient with yourself and allow

yourself to move through your emotions at your own pace.

2. Seek Support: Reach out for support from friends, family, or a therapist when you need it. Sharing your feelings can provide comfort and perspective.

3. Stay Committed: Even when it feels difficult, stay committed to your self-compassion practice. Remind yourself of the benefits and the positive impact it has on your life.

Cultivating self-compassion is a powerful and transformative practice that can significantly enhance your emotional healing after a heartbreak. By treating yourself with kindness, understanding, and care, you can build resilience, improve your self-esteem, and foster a positive and supportive relationship with yourself. Remember that self-compassion is not a one-time effort but an ongoing practice that requires patience, commitment, and self-awareness. Embrace the journey with an open heart, knowing that each step you take toward self-compassion brings you closer to healing, growth, and a deeper sense of peace and well-being.

• Rediscovering Your Worth

Heartbreak can shatter your sense of self-worth, leaving you questioning your value and doubting your abilities. When a relationship ends, it is common to feel unlovable, unworthy, and even like a failure. However, the end of a relationship does not define your worth. Rediscovering your worth is a vital part of healing and moving forward. This chapter will explore what self-worth truly means, how to rebuild it after heartbreak, and practical strategies to help you rediscover your inherent value.

Understanding Self-Worth

Self-worth is the intrinsic value you place on yourself, independent of external achievements, validation, or relationships. It is the deep-seated belief that you are valuable and deserving of love, respect, and happiness simply because you exist. Unlike self-esteem, which can fluctuate based on circumstances and accomplishments, self-worth is a stable and enduring sense of personal value.

The Importance of Self-Worth

1. Emotional Resilience: A strong

sense of self-worth helps you navigate life's challenges with greater resilience and confidence. It enables you to bounce back from setbacks and view them as opportunities for growth rather than reflections of your value.

2. Healthy Relationships: When you value yourself, you are more likely to form and maintain healthy relationships. You will set boundaries, seek partners who respect and cherish you, and avoid toxic dynamics.

3. Personal Fulfillment: Recognizing your worth allows you to pursue your passions and goals without fear of failure or the need for external

validation. It fosters a sense of fulfillment and purpose in your life.

4. Mental Well-Being: Self-worth is closely linked to mental health. When you believe in your intrinsic value, you are less likely to experience anxiety, depression, and other negative mental health outcomes.

Rebuilding Self-Worth After Heartbreak

- **Acknowledging the Impact of Heartbreak**

Heartbreak can take a significant toll on your self-worth, leading to feelings of inadequacy and self-doubt. It is essential to acknowledge the impact of the breakup on your sense of self and understand that these feelings are a natural part of the healing process.

1. Emotional Turmoil: The end of a relationship can trigger a wide range of emotions, from sadness and anger to guilt and shame. These emotions can cloud your judgment and make it challenging to see your worth clearly.

2. Self-Blame: It is common to blame yourself for the breakup, focusing on what you perceive as your faults and

mistakes. This self-blame can erode your self-worth and leave you feeling unworthy of love.

3. Identity Crisis: If your identity was closely tied to the relationship, the breakup might leave you feeling lost and unsure of who you are. Rebuilding your sense of self-worth involves rediscovering your identity independent of the relationship.

- **Steps to Rediscover Your Worth**

1. Practice Self-Compassion

Treat yourself with the same kindness and understanding you would offer a close friend going through a similar experience. Acknowledge your pain without judgment and remind yourself that it is okay to feel vulnerable and hurt.

- Self-Kindness: Offer yourself comforting words and gestures. For example, say to yourself, "It's okay to feel this way. I am going through a tough time, but I will get through this."

- Common Humanity: Remember that heartbreak is a universal experience. You are not alone in your suffering, and many others have gone through similar pain and emerged stronger.

- Mindfulness: Stay present with your emotions without letting them overwhelm you. Practice mindfulness techniques, such as deep breathing and meditation, to help you stay grounded.

2. Reflect on Your Strengths and Accomplishments

Make a conscious effort to focus on your strengths and achievements, no matter how small they may seem. Reflecting on your positive qualities and past successes can help rebuild your self-worth.

- List Your Strengths: Write down a list of your strengths and positive attributes. Include qualities such as kindness, resilience, creativity, and intelligence.

- Celebrate Your Accomplishments: Reflect on your past achievements and successes, both big and small. Celebrate these moments and recognize the effort and determination it took to accomplish them.

- Affirm Your Worth: Use positive affirmations to reinforce your sense of self-worth. Repeat affirmations such as "I am worthy of love and respect" and "I am proud of who I am."

3. Set Boundaries and Prioritize Self-Respect

Setting healthy boundaries is crucial for maintaining your self-worth. Boundaries help you protect your emotional well-being and ensure that you are treated with respect.

- Identify Your Boundaries: Reflect on what is important to you and what you need to feel safe and respected in your relationships. This might include emotional, physical, and mental boundaries.

- Communicate Clearly: Communicate your boundaries clearly and assertively to others. Remember that setting boundaries is an act of self-respect, not selfishness.

- Respect Yourself: Prioritize your needs and well-being. Make decisions that align with your values and respect your boundaries, even if it means making difficult choices.

4. Rediscover Your Passions and Interests

Reconnecting with your passions and interests can help you rediscover your sense of self and rebuild your self-worth.

- Explore New Hobbies: Try new activities and hobbies that interest you. This can help you discover new passions and provide a sense of accomplishment and joy.

- Reconnect with Old Interests: Revisit activities and interests that you enjoyed before the relationship. This can remind you of your identity outside of the relationship and reignite your enthusiasm.

- Engage in Meaningful Activities: Participate in activities that give you a sense of purpose and fulfillment. This might include volunteering, creative pursuits, or physical activities.

5. Surround Yourself with Positive Influences

The people you surround yourself with can significantly impact your self-worth. Seek out supportive and positive influences who uplift and encourage you.

- Supportive Friends and Family: Spend time with friends and family members who offer unconditional support and understanding. Their encouragement can boost your self-worth and provide a sense of belonging.

- Positive Role Models: Seek out role models who embody the qualities you admire and aspire to. Learn from their experiences and draw inspiration from their journeys.

- Limit Negative Influences: Distance yourself from individuals who are critical, unsupportive, or toxic. Negative influences can undermine your self-worth and hinder your healing process.

Practical Exercises to Enhance Self-Worth

1. Journaling

Journaling is a powerful tool for self-reflection and personal growth. Use journaling to explore your thoughts and feelings, reflect on your strengths, and set goals for rebuilding your self-worth.

- Daily Gratitude: Write down three things you are grateful for each day. Focusing on gratitude can shift your mindset from scarcity to abundance and enhance your sense of self-worth.

- Strengths and Accomplishments: Keep a journal of your strengths, positive qualities, and accomplishments. Regularly review and add to this journal to reinforce your self-worth.

- Self-Compassion Letters: Write

letters to yourself from the perspective of a compassionate friend. Offer yourself understanding, comfort, and encouragement.

2. Visualization

Visualization can help you build a positive self-image and reinforce your sense of self-worth.

- Positive Visualization: Close your eyes and visualize yourself as confident, capable, and worthy. Imagine yourself achieving your goals and living a fulfilling life.

- Future Self: Visualize your future self who has fully healed and rediscovered their worth. Imagine how you will feel, think, and behave in this future state.

3. Affirmations

Positive affirmations can help reprogram your mind and reinforce your self-worth.

- Create Affirmations: Write down affirmations that resonate with you and reflect your inherent worth. Examples include "I am deserving of love and respect" and "I am proud of who I am."

- Repeat Daily: Repeat your affirmations daily, preferably in front of a mirror. Say them with conviction and belief, allowing the positive messages to sink in.

4. Acts of Self-Love

Engaging in acts of self-love can nurture your sense of self-worth and remind you of your value.

- Self-Care Routine: Establish a self-care routine that prioritizes your physical, emotional, and mental well-being. This might include activities such as exercise, meditation, and spending time in nature.

- Treat Yourself: Treat yourself to something special that brings you joy and comfort. This could be a favorite meal, a relaxing bath, or a new book.

- Celebrate Milestones: Celebrate your milestones and achievements, no matter how small. Acknowledge the effort and progress you have made in your healing journey.

Overcoming Obstacles to Rediscovering Your Worth

- **Addressing Negative Self-Talk**

Negative self-talk can be a significant obstacle to rediscovering your worth. Challenging and transforming these thoughts is essential for rebuilding your self-esteem.

- Identify Negative Thoughts: Pay attention to your inner dialogue and identify negative thoughts as they arise. Write them down to gain clarity.

- Challenge the Thoughts: Question the validity of your negative thoughts. Ask yourself if there is evidence to support them and consider alternative perspectives.

- Replace with Positive Affirmations: Replace negative thoughts with positive affirmations that reflect your inherent worth. Practice these affirmations regularly to reinforce a positive self-image.

- **Letting Go of Perfectionism**

Perfectionism can undermine your self-worth by setting unattainably high standards and fostering a fear of failure. Embracing your imperfections is a crucial step in rediscovering your worth.

- Acknowledge Your Imperfections: Recognize that everyone makes mistakes and has flaws. Embrace your imperfections as part of what makes you unique and human.

- Set Realistic Expectations: Strive for progress, not perfection. Set achievable goals and celebrate your efforts, even if they don't always lead to the desired outcome.

- Practice Self-Compassion: Treat yourself with kindness and understanding when you fall short of your own expectations. Offer yourself the same empathy and support you would offer to a friend facing similar challenges.

- **Overcoming Comparison**

Constantly comparing yourself to others can erode your self-worth and lead to feelings of inadequacy. Learning to appreciate your own journey and accomplishments is key to overcoming the comparison trap.

- Focus on Your Journey: Shift your focus from others' achievements to your own progress and growth. Recognize that everyone's path is unique, and comparison serves no purpose.

- Gratitude Practice: Cultivate gratitude for your own strengths, opportunities, and experiences. Remind yourself of the blessings in your life and the progress you have made.

- Limit Social Media: Be mindful of how social media affects your self-worth. Limit your time on social platforms and curate your feed to include positive and inspiring content.

- **Seeking Support**

Seeking support from others can be instrumental in rediscovering your worth, especially during challenging times. Surrounding yourself with understanding and empathetic individuals can validate your feelings and provide encouragement.

- Reach Out to Loved Ones: Lean on friends, family members, or support groups for emotional support. Share your feelings and experiences with trusted individuals who uplift and validate you.

- Professional Help: Consider seeking guidance from a therapist or counselor who specializes in self-esteem and relationships. Professional support can offer valuable insights and strategies for rebuilding your self-worth.

- Joining Supportive Communities: Connect with communities or online forums where individuals share similar experiences and struggles. Engaging with others who understand can provide a sense of belonging and validation.

Embracing Your Inherent Worth

Rediscovering your worth is a journey of self-discovery, self-compassion, and personal growth. It involves letting go of self-doubt and embracing your inherent value as a unique and valuable individual. By practicing self-compassion, acknowledging your strengths, setting healthy boundaries, and surrounding yourself with positive influences, you can reclaim your sense of self-worth and move forward with confidence and resilience. Remember that your worth is not determined by external factors or the opinions of others—it resides within you, waiting to be acknowledged and celebrated. Embrace your worthiness, embrace your journey, and embrace yourself with love and acceptance.

• The Value of Talking About It

In the journey of healing a broken heart, seeking support is not just a suggestion but often a necessity. This chapter delves into the profound value of talking about your emotions, experiences, and struggles during this challenging time.

Understanding the Importance:

1. Emotional Release:

Venting out feelings, whether it's anger, sadness, or confusion, provides a cathartic release. Bottling up emotions can intensify pain and prolong the healing process. Sharing your story with a trusted friend, family member, or therapist can provide a safe space to express yourself without judgment.

2. Gaining Perspective:

Talking to others about your situation can offer fresh perspectives and insights. Sometimes, when we're deeply entrenched in our own pain, it's hard to see beyond it. Friends or professionals can offer objective viewpoints or share similar experiences that shed light on your own.

3. Validation and Empathy:

One of the most comforting aspects of seeking support is feeling validated and understood. When someone listens to your story with empathy, it validates your emotions and makes you feel less alone in your struggles. This validation can be incredibly healing and reassuring.

Who Can You Turn To:

1. Friends and Family:

Close friends and family members are often the first line of support during difficult times. They know you well and can provide unconditional love, empathy, and practical help. Whether it's a shoulder to cry on or a distraction from your pain, their presence can be immensely comforting.

2. Support Groups:

Joining a support group or online community of people who have gone through similar experiences can be incredibly beneficial. Being surrounded by individuals who understand what you're going through can provide validation, encouragement, and a sense of belonging.

3. Therapists or Counselors:

Professional support from therapists or counselors offers a unique advantage. They are trained to help you navigate complex emotions, identify unhealthy patterns, and develop coping strategies. Therapy provides a confidential space to explore your feelings without fear of judgment.

Tips for Effective Communication:

1. Be Honest and Open:

Authenticity is key when seeking support. Be honest about your feelings and experiences, even if they are difficult to articulate. Transparency fosters deeper connections and allows others to understand you better.

2. Set Boundaries:

While it's important to open up, it's equally important to set boundaries to protect your emotional well-being. Only share what you feel comfortable sharing, and don't feel obligated to divulge every detail if it makes you uncomfortable.

3. Listen and Reciprocate:

Support is a two-way street. While it's important to express your own feelings, also be willing to listen to others and offer support in return. Building reciprocal relationships fosters mutual trust and strengthens bonds.

Seeking support is not a sign of weakness but a courageous step towards healing. Whether it's through conversations with loved ones, joining support groups, or seeking professional help, talking about your emotions can be a transformative process. Remember, you don't have to go through this journey alone. Reach out, lean on others, and allow yourself to be supported on the path to healing your broken heart.

• Finding a Support System

In the aftermath of heartbreak, finding a support system is like discovering an oasis in the desert – a source of comfort, sustenance, and rejuvenation amidst the arid landscape of emotional turmoil. This chapter delves into the art of building a robust support system tailored to your needs and circumstances.

The Importance of a Support System:

1. Emotional Stability:

A support system provides a stabilizing force during tumultuous times. When your world feels like it's crumbling, having dependable individuals to lean on can prevent you from spiraling into despair.

2. Validation and Empathy:

Sharing your pain with others who understand and empathize with your experience can be incredibly validating.

Knowing that you're not alone in your struggles fosters a sense of belonging and reassurance.

3. Practical Assistance:

Beyond emotional support, a solid support system can offer practical help with everyday tasks or decision-making. Whether it's helping you move out of your shared home, providing childcare, or assisting with finances, having reliable allies can ease the burden of navigating life post-breakup.

Building Your Support System:

1. Identify Trusted Individuals:

Start by identifying people in your life

whom you trust and feel comfortable confiding in. This could include close friends, family members, mentors, or even colleagues who have demonstrated empathy and understanding.

2. Diversify Your Network:

While close friends and family are essential pillars of support, don't underestimate the value of expanding your network. Joining support groups, attending therapy sessions, or engaging with online communities can connect you with individuals who share similar experiences and perspectives.

3. Communicate Your Needs:

Be clear about what kind of support you need from each person in your support system. Whether it's a listening ear, a distraction from your pain, or practical assistance, communicate your needs openly and honestly.

Nurturing Your Support System:

1. Reciprocity:

Support is a reciprocal exchange. While it's important to lean on others during difficult times, don't forget to reciprocate their support when they need it. Cultivating mutually supportive relationships strengthens bonds and fosters a sense of community.

2. Boundaries:

Set boundaries to protect your emotional well-being within your support system. Be clear about what you're comfortable sharing and receiving, and don't hesitate to enforce boundaries if they're being crossed.

3. Self-Care:

While support from others is invaluable, self-care remains paramount. Nurture yourself physically, emotionally, and spiritually to maintain resilience and prevent burnout.

Remember that you are your own most important ally in the journey of healing.

Building a support system is not just about finding people to lean on; it's about cultivating meaningful connections that nurture your growth and well-being. Whether through trusted friends, family members, therapists, or support groups, your support system can provide the scaffolding you need to navigate the complexities of healing a broken heart. Invest time and effort into nurturing these relationships, and you'll find yourself buoyed by the collective strength of those who care for you.

Chapter 5

Moving Forward

• Setting New Goals

After the storm of heartbreak, the path to healing begins with forward momentum. This chapter explores the transformative power of setting new goals as a catalyst for personal growth, empowerment, and renewal.

Embracing Change:

1. Acknowledging the Shift:

Heartbreak often marks the end of one chapter and the beginning of another. Embrace this transition as an opportunity for reinvention and self-discovery. Recognize that while the pain of the past may linger, it doesn't define your future.

2. Letting Go of the Past:

Setting new goals requires releasing attachments to the past – whether it's lingering feelings for your ex-partner, regrets, or what-ifs. By letting go of what no longer serves you, you create space for new possibilities to emerge.

The Power of Goal Setting:

1. Clarity and Focus:

Setting goals provides a roadmap for navigating the uncertain terrain of post -breakup life. It offers clarity amidst chaos and a sense of purpose to guide your actions forward. Define what you want to achieve and create actionable steps to get there.

2. Empowerment and Agency:

Taking control of your destiny through goal setting empowers you to reclaim agency over your life. Instead of feeling like a passive victim of circumstance, you become the architect of your own future. Set goals that resonate with your values, passions, and aspirations.

Types of Goals to Consider:

1. Personal Growth:

Invest in self-improvement by setting goals that nurture your mental, emotional, and spiritual well-being. This could involve learning new skills, cultivating healthy habits, or exploring creative outlets that bring you joy.

2. Career and Education:

Channel your energy into advancing your career or educational pursuits. Set professional goals that align with your long-term aspirations, whether it's climbing the corporate ladder, starting your own business, or pursuing further education.

3. Health and Wellness:

Prioritize your physical and mental health by setting goals related to exercise, nutrition, stress management, and self-care. Establishing a holistic wellness routine can boost your resilience and vitality as you navigate life's challenges.

Overcoming Obstacles:

1. Fear of Failure:

Don't let the fear of failure paralyze you. Setbacks are inevitable on the path to achieving your goals, but they also present opportunities for growth and learning. Embrace failure as a natural part of the process and persevere in the face of adversity.

2. Self-Doubt and Limiting Beliefs:

Challenge self-limiting beliefs that undermine your confidence and potential. Cultivate a growth mindset that acknowledges your capacity for growth and resilience. Surround yourself with positive influences that uplift and encourage you on your journey.

Celebrating Progress:

1. Milestones and Achievements:

Celebrate each step forward, no matter how small. Acknowledge your progress and achievements as markers of resilience and perseverance. Take pride in your growth and use it as fuel to propel you further along your path.

2. Self-Reflection:

Regularly reflect on your goals, progress, and priorities. Adjust your course as needed to stay aligned with your evolving aspirations and values. Remember that the journey of healing and growth is not linear but marked by twists, turns, and detours.

Setting new goals is not just about moving on from the past; it's about embracing the infinite possibilities of the future. By envisioning and pursuing your dreams with purpose and determination, you reclaim agency over your narrative and redefine what it means to thrive after heartbreak. As you embark on this journey of self-discovery and transformation, may you find solace, strength, and inspiration in the pursuit of your aspirations.

• Embracing Change

Embracing change is akin to navigating uncharted waters—it's both daunting and exhilarating. In the realm of healing a broken heart, it becomes not just a necessity but a lifeline. Change is the catalyst for growth, the gentle push that propels us forward when we feel stuck in the quagmire of heartache.

At its core, embracing change involves a profound shift in perspective. It's about acknowledging that while the past may have shaped us, it doesn't define us. It's about recognizing that the pain we feel today doesn't have to dictate our tomorrows. Instead, it offers an opportunity for renewal, for rediscovering who we are and what we're capable of.

But change isn't always a welcome guest. It can be uncomfortable, unsettling, even frightening. It requires us to step outside our comfort zones, to confront the unknown with a courage we didn't know we possessed. Yet, within the crucible of change lies the potential for profound transformation.

One of the most remarkable aspects of embracing change is its ability to reveal our resilience. It forces us to dig deep, to tap into reservoirs of strength we never knew existed. It teaches us that we are far more adaptable than we give ourselves credit for, that we have the capacity to weather even the stormiest of seas.

Moreover, embracing change invites us to surrender to the natural ebb and flow of life. It reminds us that change is inevitable, that trying to cling to the past is like trying to grasp water—it slips through our fingers, leaving us empty-handed and longing for what once was. Instead, we must learn to ride the waves of change, to trust in the currents that carry us ever onward.

In the context of healing a broken heart, embracing change means letting go of what no longer serves us. It means releasing the grip of bitterness and resentment, of sorrow and regret. It means opening ourselves up to the possibility of love, even when it feels like the most terrifying thing in the world.

Ultimately, embracing change is an act of faith—a belief that no matter how dark the night may seem, dawn will always break. It's a testament to the indomitable human spirit, to our capacity for growth and renewal in the face of adversity. And in the journey of healing a broken heart, it is the guiding light that leads us back to ourselves, whole and unbroken once more.

• Learning to Love Again

Learning to love again is like embarking on a journey through uncharted territory—a path fraught with twists and turns, highs and lows, but ultimately leading to the profound discovery of the heart's resilience. In the wake of heartbreak, the idea of opening oneself up to love once more can seem like an insurmountable task, akin to scaling the highest peak or traversing the deepest chasm. Yet, it is precisely in this act of vulnerability that the true essence of healing resides.

At its essence, learning to love again is a process of self-discovery—a journey inward to unearth the buried treasure of our own capacity for love. It requires us to peel back the layers of pain and disappointment, to confront the wounds of the past with a courage born of self-awareness and introspection. It is a journey of rediscovery, of reclaiming the parts of ourselves we may have lost along the way.

But learning to love again is not just about looking inward—it's also about reaching outward, extending a hand of compassion and understanding to those who may have hurt us in the past. It's about recognizing that forgiveness is not just a gift we give to others, but a gift we give to ourselves—a release from the burden of resentment and anger that weighs heavy on the soul.

Moreover, learning to love again means embracing the unknown with a sense of openness and curiosity. It means relinquishing the need for certainty and control, and instead surrendering to the unpredictable currents of the heart. It means being willing to take risks, to leap into the abyss of possibility with a faith that the universe will catch us when we fall.

In healing a broken heart, learning to love again is a testament to the indomitable human spirit. It's a declaration of resilience, a refusal to let past pain define our future happiness. It's a recognition that while scars may linger, they do not have the power to dictate the course of our lives.

But perhaps most importantly, learning to love again is an act of profound courage. It's a willingness to embrace the inherent vulnerability of the human experience, to lay bare our hearts in the hope that they will be met with kindness and understanding. It's a recognition that true love is not without risk, but that the rewards far outweigh the potential pitfalls.

In the end, learning to love again is a journey worth taking—a journey that leads not only to the healing of a broken heart, but to the discovery of a love that is deeper, stronger, and more resilient than we ever imagined possible. And it is in this journey that we find not only solace, but redemption—a testament to the enduring power of the human heart to heal, to forgive, and to love again.

Chapter 6

Forgiveness and Letting Go

• The Power of Forgiveness

The power of forgiveness is like a beacon of light in the darkest of nights. It holds within it the transformative ability to heal wounds, mend broken relationships, and set souls free. In the context of healing a broken heart, forgiveness plays a pivotal role in the journey towards inner peace and emotional liberation.

At its core, forgiveness is a conscious decision to release feelings of resentment, anger, and bitterness towards someone who has caused us pain. It is not an easy task, as it requires us to confront and acknowledge the hurt that we have experienced. However, the act of forgiveness is not just a gift that we bestow upon others; it is also a gift that we give ourselves.

When we hold onto grudges and refuse to forgive, we carry the weight of those negative emotions within us like a heavy burden. They weigh us down, draining our energy and poisoning our hearts. But when we choose to forgive, we relinquish that burden, allowing ourselves to experience a profound sense of relief and liberation.

Forgiveness is not synonymous with forgetting or condoning the actions that caused us pain. It does not mean that we have to reconcile with the person who hurt us or pretend that the hurt never occurred. Rather, forgiveness is about letting go of the hold that the past has over us. It is about refusing to let our pain define us or dictate our future.

In healing a broken heart, forgiveness is often a necessary step towards moving forward. It allows us to break free from the cycle of resentment and anger that keeps us tethered to the past. By forgiving those who have hurt us, we create space within ourselves for healing to take place. We open ourselves up to the possibility of healing old wounds and making room for new growth and happiness.

Forgiveness is also a deeply personal journey. It is something that we must do for ourselves, regardless of whether the person who hurt us acknowledges their wrongdoing or seeks our forgiveness. It is about reclaiming our power and taking control of our own emotional well-being.

Moreover, forgiveness is a process rather than a one-time event. It may take time and effort to fully forgive someone, especially if the pain they caused runs deep. It requires patience, self-reflection, and sometimes even professional guidance. But with perseverance and a willingness to let go of the past, forgiveness can lead us towards profound healing and transformation.

The power of forgiveness is unparalleled in its ability to mend broken hearts and restore inner peace. It is a courageous act of self-love that allows us to release the pain of the past and embrace the promise of a brighter future. By choosing forgiveness, we unlock the door to healing and reclaim our joy, our strength, and our freedom.

• Letting Go of Resentment

Letting go of resentment is a crucial aspect of healing a broken heart.

Resentment is like a poison that slowly corrodes the soul, keeping us tethered to the pain of the past and preventing us from moving forward. In order to truly heal, we must learn to release this toxic emotion and make room for healing, growth, and happiness.

Resentment often stems from feelings of betrayal, injustice, or hurt inflicted by others. It can manifest as anger, bitterness, or a desire for revenge. Holding onto resentment keeps us trapped in a cycle of negativity, replaying past grievances in our minds and allowing them to fester and grow.

However, the act of letting go of

resentment is not about excusing or forgetting the wrongs that have been done to us. It is about acknowledging our pain, validating our emotions, and choosing to release the grip that the past has on us. It is a conscious decision to free ourselves from the burden of carrying around unresolved anger and resentment.

One of the first steps in letting go of resentment is to recognize the toll that it is taking on our own well-being. Holding onto resentment does not harm the person who has wronged us; instead, it only serves to poison our own hearts and minds. It affects our mental and emotional health, leading to increased stress, anxiety, and even physical symptoms such as headaches or insomnia.

Once we understand the detrimental effects of resentment, we can begin the process of letting it go. This often involves practicing self-awareness and mindfulness, tuning into our emotions and recognizing when resentment begins to surface. By acknowledging these feelings without judgment, we can begin to diffuse their power over us.

Another important aspect of letting go of resentment is practicing empathy and compassion towards ourselves and others. This does not mean that we have to condone or justify the actions of those who have hurt us; rather, it is about recognizing the humanity in both ourselves and others. We are all imperfect beings capable of making mistakes, and holding onto resentment only perpetuates a cycle of hurt and suffering.

Forgiveness is also a key component of letting go of resentment. Forgiveness is not about letting the other person off the hook or pretending that the hurt never occurred; rather, it is about releasing the hold that the past has on us and reclaiming our power to live in the present moment. Forgiveness is a gift that we give to ourselves, allowing us to break free from the chains of resentment and find peace within ourselves.

Letting go of resentment is a process that takes time, patience, and self-reflection. It may involve seeking support from loved ones, therapy, or other forms of self-care. But with dedication and perseverance, it is possible to release the grip of resentment and open ourselves up to a future filled with healing, love, and joy.

• Moving Past the Pain

Moving past the pain of a broken heart is a journey that can be both challenging and rewarding. It's a process of self-discovery, growth, and ultimately, healing. Here's a detailed exploration of how to navigate through this difficult time and emerge stronger on the other side:

1. Acknowledge Your Feelings: The first step in moving past the pain is to acknowledge and accept your feelings. It's okay to feel sad, angry, or even lost. Allow yourself to experience these

emotions without judgment.

2. Grieve the Loss: Healing cannot begin until you've allowed yourself to grieve the loss of the relationship. Take the time to mourn the end of something that was meaningful to you.

3. Seek Support: Surround yourself with supportive friends and family who can offer a listening ear and a shoulder to lean on. Don't hesitate to seek professional help if you need it.

4. Practice Self-Care: Take care of yourself both mentally and physically. Engage in activities that bring you joy and relaxation, whether it's exercise,

meditation, or pursuing a hobby.

5. Reflect on the Relationship: Use this time to reflect on the relationship and what you've learned from it. What were the positives and negatives? What patterns or behaviors do you want to avoid in future relationships?

6. Forgive Yourself and Your Ex: Forgiveness is a powerful tool in the healing process. Forgive yourself for any mistakes you may have made, and forgive your ex for theirs. Holding onto resentment will only prolong your pain.

7. Let Go of Resentment: Holding onto resentment towards your ex will only

hinder your ability to move forward. Letting go of resentment doesn't mean you have to forget what happened, but it does mean releasing the negative emotions associated with it.

8. Focus on the Present: Instead of dwelling on the past or worrying about the future, focus on the present moment. Practice mindfulness and gratitude to appreciate the beauty and joy in your life right now.

9. Set Boundaries: If necessary, set boundaries with your ex to protect yourself emotionally. This might mean limiting contact or avoiding certain places or activities that remind you of

them.

10. Rediscover Yourself: Use this time to reconnect with yourself and rediscover your passions, interests, and goals. Invest in self-improvement and personal growth.

11. Stay Open to Love: While it's important to take the time to heal, don't close yourself off to the possibility of love in the future. Keep an open heart and mind, and trust that when the time is right, love will find you again.

12. Celebrate Your Progress: Celebrate each small victory along the way.

Whether it's going a day without thinking about your ex or trying something new, acknowledge and celebrate your progress.

13. Seek Closure: Closure can be an important part of the healing process. If you feel it's necessary, have a conversation with your ex to gain closure and clarity.

14. Stay Patient: Healing from a broken heart takes time, so be patient with yourself. Allow yourself to heal at your own pace and trust that you will eventually emerge from this experience stronger and wiser.

15. Embrace the Future: Finally, embrace the future with optimism and excitement. Use this experience as an opportunity for growth and transformation, and believe that brighter days are ahead.

Moving past the pain of a broken heart is never easy, but with time, patience, and self-love, it is possible to heal and move forward towards a happier and more fulfilling life.

Chapter 7

Rediscovering Joy

• Pursuing Passions and Hobbies

Exploring passions and hobbies can be a transformative part of healing a broken heart. Here's an in-depth look at how immersing yourself in activities you love can help you navigate through the pain and find joy and fulfillment:

1. Discovering New Passions:

Often, when we're in a relationship, we may neglect our individual interests or put them on hold. Use this time to explore new passions and hobbies that you may have always been curious about but never had the chance to pursue.

2. Rediscovering Old Hobbies:

Alternatively, reconnecting with hobbies and activities you enjoyed before the relationship can be incredibly comforting and grounding. Revisit old hobbies with fresh eyes and a renewed sense of enthusiasm.

3. Creative Outlets:

Engaging in creative pursuits such as painting, writing, or playing music can be cathartic and therapeutic. Use art as a means of expressing your emotions and processing your feelings in a healthy way.

4. Physical Activities:

Physical activities like hiking, dancing, or yoga not only benefit your physical health but also boost your mood and reduce stress. Exercise releases endorphins, which are natural mood lifters, helping to alleviate feelings of sadness and anxiety.

5. Social Hobbies:

Joining clubs or groups centered around shared interests can provide a sense of community and belonging, which is especially beneficial during times of heartbreak. Whether it's a book club, a sports team, or a cooking class, connecting with others who share your passions can be uplifting and empowering.

6. Solo Pursuits:

On the other hand, solo hobbies such as gardening, knitting, or photography offer moments of solitude and self-reflection, allowing you to reconnect with yourself and find inner peace.

7. Learning New Skills:

Use this time to invest in self-improvement by learning new skills or taking up a new hobby. Whether it's learning a new language, mastering a musical instrument, or honing your cooking skills, the process of learning and growth can be incredibly fulfilling and empowering.

8. Setting Goals:

Pursuing passions and hobbies gives you something to work towards and look forward to, which can be particularly valuable when you're feeling lost or aimless. Set small, achievable goals for yourself within your hobbies, and celebrate your progress along the way.

9. Distraction and Relaxation:

Immersing yourself in activities you enjoy can provide a much-needed distraction from the pain of heartbreak. It gives you something positive to focus on and helps alleviate stress and anxiety.

10. Building Confidence and Self-Esteem:

Accomplishing goals and mastering new skills boosts your confidence and self-esteem, which are often shaken by the end of a relationship. Engaging in hobbies that make you feel competent and capable reminds you of your worth and strengths.

11. Finding Meaning and Purpose:

Pursuing passions and hobbies can give your life a sense of meaning and purpose beyond romantic relationships. It reminds you that there is so much more to life than just love, and that you are capable of finding fulfillment and happiness on your own.

12. Time for Self-Reflection:

Hobbies provide an opportunity for introspection and self-discovery. Use this time to reflect on your values, goals, and priorities, and consider how you want to shape your life moving forward.

13. Embracing Joy and Fun:

Ultimately, pursuing passions and hobbies is about embracing joy and having fun. Allow yourself to experience moments of pure happiness and pleasure, even amidst the pain of heartbreak.

14. Balance and Moderation:

While diving into hobbies can be incredibly therapeutic, it's important to maintain balance and moderation.

Avoid using hobbies as a means of escapism or distraction to the point where you're neglecting other aspects of your life.

15. Celebrating Self-Love:

Engaging in activities that bring you joy and fulfillment is an act of self-love. It's a reminder that you are deserving of happiness and that your well-being is worth investing in.

Pursuing passions and hobbies is a powerful tool for healing a broken heart. Whether you're discovering new interests, reconnecting with old hobbies, or setting goals for self-improvement, immersing yourself in activities you love can bring joy, fulfillment, and a sense of purpose to your life, helping you navigate through the pain of heartbreak and emerge stronger and more resilient on the other side.

• Reconnecting with Joyful Activities

Reconnecting with joyful activities is a vital step in the healing process after experiencing a broken heart. While it may initially seem daunting or even impossible to find joy in the midst of pain, engaging in activities that bring you happiness can gradually help uplift your spirits and restore a sense of normalcy to your life.

First and foremost, it's important to acknowledge that healing takes time and patience. Be gentle with yourself and allow yourself to grieve. However, as you begin to navigate through the healing process, incorporating joyful activities into your routine can serve as a beacon of light amidst the darkness.

One approach is to revisit hobbies or interests that you may have neglected during the course of your relationship.

Whether it's painting, writing, gardening, or playing a musical instrument, immersing yourself in activities that once brought you joy can reignite your passion and provide a much-needed sense of fulfillment.

Additionally, consider exploring new activities or hobbies that pique your interest. This could involve taking up a new sport, joining a book club, or learning a new skill such as cooking or photography. By stepping outside of your comfort zone and embracing new experiences, you not only distract yourself from the pain but also open yourself up to a world of possibilities and growth.

Furthermore, connecting with nature can be incredibly healing. Spending time outdoors, whether it's going for a hike, taking a leisurely stroll in the park, or simply sitting by the ocean, can help soothe your soul and provide a sense of peace and tranquility. Nature has a way of reminding us of the beauty and wonder of the world, even in the midst of our darkest moments.

Moreover, don't underestimate the power of laughter. Surround yourself with loved ones who bring positivity and humor into your life. Whether it's sharing funny stories, watching a comedy show, or simply enjoying each other's company, laughter has a remarkable ability to lift your spirits and remind you that joy still exists, even in the midst of pain.

Finally, practicing self-care is essential in the healing process. This involves prioritizing your physical, emotional, and mental well-being. Whether it's getting enough sleep, eating nourishing foods, or engaging in relaxation techniques such as meditation or yoga, taking care of yourself lays the foundation for healing and allows you to fully embrace and enjoy the activities that bring you joy.

Reconnecting with joyful activities is a crucial aspect of healing a broken heart. By engaging in hobbies, exploring new experiences, connecting with nature, surrounding yourself with positivity, and practicing self-care, you can gradually begin to find solace, hope, and happiness once again. Remember, healing is a journey, and each step you take towards joy brings you closer to wholeness and healing.

• Celebrating Small Victories

Celebrating small victories is an integral part of the healing process when overcoming a broken heart. In the midst of pain and heartache, it's easy to feel overwhelmed and defeated. However, recognizing and commemorating the small triumphs along the way can provide a much-needed sense of progress, accomplishment, and hope.

One of the first steps in celebrating small victories is acknowledging your emotions and allowing yourself to feel them fully. Healing from a broken heart is a journey, and it's important to give yourself credit for every step you take, no matter how small. Whether it's getting out of bed in the morning, reaching out to a friend for support, or simply making it through the day, each action represents a victory in itself.

Moreover, setting achievable goals can help provide direction and motivation during the healing process. These goals can be as simple as going for a walk, trying out a new recipe, or finishing a work project. By breaking down larger tasks into smaller, manageable steps, you create opportunities for success and progress, which can boost your confidence and self-esteem.

Additionally, practicing self-compassion is crucial when celebrating small victories. Be kind to yourself and recognize that healing takes time. It's okay to have setbacks along the way; what matters is that you continue to persevere and acknowledge your progress, no matter how small. Treat yourself with the same kindness and encouragement that you would offer to a friend going through a similar situation.

Furthermore, surrounding yourself with a supportive network of friends and loved ones can amplify the joy of celebrating small victories. Share your successes with those who care about you, and allow them to celebrate alongside you. Whether it's a congratulatory text, a heartfelt conversation, or a small gesture of kindness, the support of others can make your victories feel even more meaningful.

Moreover, finding gratitude in the little things can significantly impact your ability to celebrate small victories. Take a moment each day to reflect on the things you're grateful for, whether it's a beautiful sunset, a kind gesture from a stranger, or a moment of peace and quiet. Cultivating an attitude of gratitude can shift your perspective and help you find joy in even the most challenging circumstances.

Remember to celebrate yourself. Treat yourself to something special as a reward for your hard work and perseverance. Whether it's indulging in your favorite meal, treating yourself to a spa day, or simply taking some time to relax and unwind, honoring yourself for your achievements is essential in fostering a sense of self-worth and empowerment.

Celebrating small victories is a powerful tool in the healing process after experiencing a broken heart. By acknowledging your progress, setting achievable goals, practicing self-compassion, seeking support from others, finding gratitude, and honoring yourself, you can cultivate a sense of resilience, hope, and joy as you navigate through the journey of healing. Remember, every small victory brings you one step closer to wholeness and happiness.

Chapter 8

Embracing New Beginnings

• Opening Your Heart Again

Opening your heart again after experiencing the pain of a broken heart is a profound and courageous act. It's like standing at the edge of a cliff, feeling the fear of falling yet being drawn to the breathtaking view beyond. It requires vulnerability, forgiveness, and a willingness to trust in the face of uncertainty.

Opening your heart again begins with self-awareness and acceptance. It's about acknowledging the hurt and pain you've endured, but also recognizing that those experiences do not define you. You are not broken; you are simply wounded, and wounds heal with time and care.

Forgiveness plays a crucial role in the process of opening your heart again. This includes forgiving yourself for any mistakes you may have made and forgiving others for any pain they may have caused you. Holding onto resentment and anger only serves to keep your heart closed off from the possibility of love and connection.

To open your heart again, you must be willing to take risks and embrace vulnerability. This means letting down the walls you've built around your heart and allowing yourself to be seen, flaws and all. It may feel scary at first, but it's through vulnerability that deep connections are formed.

Practice self-love and self-care as you navigate the journey of opening your heart again. Treat yourself with kindness and compassion, and surround yourself with people who uplift and support you. Engage in activities that bring you joy and fulfillment, and nurture your mind, body, and soul.

Be patient with yourself and with the process. Healing takes time, and opening your heart again is not something that happens overnight. It's a gradual unfolding, a journey of growth and discovery. Allow yourself to feel all the emotions that come up along the way – the joy, the sadness, the fear, and the hope.

Above all, trust in the power of love. Trust that despite the pain you've experienced in the past, love is still worth pursuing. Trust that you are deserving of love, and that love will find its way back to you when the time is right. Open your heart again, and allow yourself to experience the beauty and magic of love in all its forms.

• Building Healthy Relationships

In the journey of healing a broken heart, building healthy relationships becomes not just a goal but also a vital part of the healing process itself. Healthy relationships offer support, understanding, and companionship, helping to mend the wounds left behind by heartbreak and fostering a sense of connection and belonging. Here's a deep dive into the art of building healthy relationships:

1. Self-Reflection: Before diving into new relationships, it's essential to take the time for self-reflection. Understand your own needs, desires, and boundaries. Reflect on past relationships to identify patterns and lessons learned. Self-awareness lays the foundation for healthy connections with others.

2. Communication: Healthy

relationships thrive on open, honest communication. Express your thoughts, feelings, and needs clearly and respectfully. Be an active listener, giving the other person your full attention and validating their experiences. Effective communication builds trust and strengthens bonds.

3. Trust: Trust is the cornerstone of any healthy relationship. It develops over time through consistency, reliability, and honesty. Be trustworthy by keeping your promises, being transparent, and honoring your commitments. Trust also involves giving others the benefit of the doubt

and believing in their intentions.

4. Respect: Respect is fundamental to healthy relationships. It involves valuing the other person's opinions, boundaries, and autonomy. Treat others with kindness, empathy, and consideration, even when you disagree. Respect also means respecting yourself and setting boundaries to protect your well-being.

5. Empathy: Empathy is the ability to understand and share the feelings of others. Cultivate empathy by actively listening, acknowledging the other person's emotions, and showing compassion. Put yourself in their

shoes and strive to see things from their perspective. Empathy fosters deeper connections and mutual understanding.

6. Boundaries: Setting and respecting boundaries is essential for maintaining healthy relationships. Boundaries define what is acceptable and unacceptable behavior and help create a sense of safety and respect. Communicate your boundaries clearly and assertively, and respect the boundaries of others. Healthy boundaries promote mutual respect and prevent resentment and conflict.

7. Compromise: Healthy relationships

involve compromise and flexibility. Be willing to negotiate and find solutions that meet the needs of both parties. Focus on finding common ground and working together as a team. Compromise strengthens relationships and fosters a sense of cooperation and mutual support.

8. Quality Time: Spending quality time together is essential for nurturing healthy relationships. Make an effort to prioritize meaningful interactions and shared experiences. Engage in activities that bring you closer together and foster connection and intimacy. Quality time builds bonds

and creates lasting memories.

9. Support:bHealthy relationships are built on a foundation of mutual support and encouragement. Be there for each other during both good times and bad, offering a listening ear, emotional support, and practical assistance. Celebrate each other's successes and provide comfort and reassurance during difficult times. Support strengthens relationships and creates a sense of security and trust.

10. Continuous Growth: Finally, healthy relationships require ongoing effort and growth. Be willing to learn from your experiences, communicate

openly about your needs and concerns, and adapt to changes together. Celebrate your successes, learn from your challenges, and continue to invest in the health and longevity of your relationships. Continuous growth fosters resilience and deepens the connection between partners.

Building healthy relationships becomes not just a destination but also a source of strength, healing, and joy. By cultivating trust, respect, empathy, and communication, you can create meaningful connections that support you on your path to healing and wholeness.

• Trusting in the Future

Trusting in the future after experiencing the pain of a broken heart can feel like navigating through a dense fog with no clear path ahead. It's natural to feel hesitant, uncertain, and even fearful of what lies ahead. However, embracing trust in the future is an essential step in the journey of healing, growth, and ultimately finding happiness again.

1. Acknowledging the Pain: Before you can trust in the future, it's important to acknowledge and process the pain of

your past experiences. Allow yourself to grieve the loss, whether it's the end of a relationship, the betrayal of trust, or the disappointment of unmet expectations. Give yourself permission to feel all the emotions that come with heartbreak – sadness, anger, loneliness, and despair. By confronting and accepting your pain, you can begin to release its grip on your heart and create space for healing.

2. Finding Meaning: As you heal from heartbreak, seek to find meaning in your experiences. Reflect on the lessons learned, the growth achieved, and the strength discovered within

yourself. Every challenge offers an opportunity for growth and transformation if you're willing to embrace it. Trust that even in the darkest moments, there is a silver lining waiting to be discovered.

3. Cultivating Self-Compassion: Trusting in the future begins with cultivating self-compassion and kindness toward yourself. Treat yourself with the same love, understanding, and forgiveness that you would offer to a dear friend. Recognize that you are deserving of happiness, love, and fulfillment, regardless of past mistakes or

setbacks. Be gentle with yourself as you navigate the ups and downs of the healing journey.

4. Letting Go of Control: One of the biggest obstacles to trusting in the future is the desire to control outcomes and avoid future pain. However, trying to control every aspect of your life only leads to stress, anxiety, and frustration. Instead, practice surrendering to the natural flow of life and trusting that everything will unfold as it's meant to. Let go of the need for certainty and embrace the beauty of uncertainty, knowing that it holds endless possibilities for growth and

discovery.

5. Fostering Hope: Trusting in the future requires cultivating a sense of hope and optimism. Focus on the possibilities that lie ahead rather than dwelling on past disappointments. Visualize the life you want to create for yourself, and believe wholeheartedly that it is within your reach. Surround yourself with people who uplift and inspire you, and seek out activities that bring you joy and fulfillment. By nourishing hope within yourself, you can cultivate a positive outlook on the future and attract abundance into your life.

6. Building Resilience: Trusting in the future also involves building resilience – the ability to bounce back from adversity stronger than before. View challenges as opportunities for growth and development rather than insurmountable obstacles. Draw upon your inner strength, courage, and perseverance to overcome obstacles and keep moving forward. Remember that setbacks are temporary, but your resilience is enduring.

7. Seeking Support: Finally, trust in the future is strengthened by seeking support from others. Surround yourself with friends, family, or a

therapist who can offer encouragement, guidance, and perspective. Share your hopes, fears, and dreams with trusted confidants who can provide a listening ear and a shoulder to lean on. Lean on your support network during difficult times, and allow their love and encouragement to bolster your faith in the future.

Trusting in the future after a broken heart is not always easy, but it is essential for moving forward and embracing the possibilities that lie ahead. By acknowledging your pain, finding meaning in your experiences, cultivating self-compassion, letting go of control, fostering hope, building resilience, and seeking support, you can begin to rebuild trust in yourself, in others, and in the beautiful journey that awaits you.

Conclusion

Before you close this book, it's important to reflect on the transformative journey you've embarked upon. Healing is not a destination but rather a continuous process—an ongoing evolution of the heart, mind, and soul.

Throughout these pages, we've explored various strategies, insights, and perspectives to support you on your healing journey. From navigating the depths of pain and grief to rediscovering joy and self-love, you've faced each challenge with courage and resilience.

But healing is not just about overcoming adversity; it's about embracing the full spectrum of human experience—the highs and lows, the love and loss, the growth and transformation. It's about recognizing that your heartache does not define you but rather serves as a catalyst for profound inner change.

As you close this chapter of your life and step into the next, remember that you are not alone. You are part of a vast community of souls who have experienced heartache and found their way back to wholeness. Draw strength from their stories, their wisdom, and their resilience.

Embrace the lessons learned from your journey—the moments of pain that shaped you, the insights that awakened you, and the love that sustained you. Carry these lessons forward as you continue to grow, evolve, and thrive.

And above all, remember to be gentle with yourself. Healing is a nonlinear process, and there will be days when the pain feels overwhelming and the progress feels slow. But in those moments, lean into the support of your loved ones, your community, and yourself.

As you navigate the twists and turns of your healing journey, trust in your inner resilience, your innate capacity for growth, and your unwavering spirit. Know that healing is not about erasing the past but rather integrating it into the fabric of your being, weaving together the threads of pain and joy to create a tapestry of wholeness.

May you continue to walk this path with courage, compassion, and grace. May you honor the resilience of your spirit and the depth of your heart. And may you emerge from this journey stronger, wiser, and more radiant than

ever before.